MACHINE LEARNING   ARCHITEC
OF ARTIFICIAL INTELLIGENCE

MACHINE
MACHINE
MACHINE
MACHINE
LEARNING
LEARNING
LEARNING

RIBA ⚜   Phil Bernstein

© Phil Bernstein, 2022

Published by RIBA Publishing, 66 Portland Place, London, W1B 1AD

ISBN 9781 85946 401 3

The right of Phil Bernstein to be identified as the Author of this Work
has been asserted in accordance with the Copyright, Designs and
Patents Act 1988 sections 77 and 78.

British Library Cataloguing-in-Publication Data

A catalogue record for this book is available from the British Library.

Commissioning Editor: Clare Holloway

Assistant Editor: Scarlet Furness

Production: Richard Blackburn

Interiors designed and typeset by Studio Kalinka

Printed and bound by TJ Books, Cornwall

Cover design: The First 47

www.ribapublishing.com

MIX
Paper from
responsible sources
FSC® C013056

ACKNOWLEDGEMENTS

When RIBA reached out to ask whether I might be interested in writing a book about the implications of artificial intelligence for the architecture profession, I was surprised to learn that another far-better known pundit (who shall remain unnamed) had declined a similar offer; apparently, the prospects, to him, were simply too dire. However, as the science-fiction writer William Gibson, of *The Difference Engine* fame, is purported to have said, 'the future is already here, it's just not evenly distributed'. Such is the case with the emergent technologies of AI, which lives on the smartphones (and thereby in the pockets) of the same architects who will be made redundant by our erstwhile robotic overlords.

What I did not realise as I started the project was that it would require me to return to my computational roots from decades ago, when I was an undergraduate student of an iconoclastic young professor at Yale, Roger Schank, who had some of the earliest foundational ideas for teaching computers to understand language. During my graduate studies, computing was emergent but largely unacknowledged, and my instructor at the time, Bob Frew, indulged my interest in using early computers (which were hardly up to any useful graphic task) for project management. Late in my final graduate year while on vacation in California, my uncle Edward Bernstein, always one to have the latest gadget, gave me a week with his brand-new Apple II Plus, on which was a new piece of software called VisiCalc, the first spreadsheet. Suddenly, numeric modelling no longer required hard coding and I surprised Bob with a finished project right after the holiday. Two years later in San Francisco, the architect Herb McLaughlin sent me several times to Palo Alto, to research a new technology called 'expert systems', a provocative but otherwise completely unrealisable technology. Around the same time, I bought his firm's first personal computer – not for generating drawings, but to manage schedules and fee proposals. Computing to generate forms and images, I came to realise, is irresistible, but digital tools have just as much, if not more, agency in architectural process outside of design itself.

After a dozen years in mainstream practice with César Pelli and his managing partner, Fred Clarke, I joined Autodesk as a vice-president, and established there many of the relationships in the technology world that I maintain today. Jim Lynch, now a senior vice-president, is a close friend, sounding board and source of much help and insight from the company. Sam Omans, now an industry manager with Autodesk's Architecture/Engineering/Construction business (and likely one of the few folks working in tech with a PhD in architectural theory) has helped clarify ideas, locate information with the Autodesk labyrinth and chase down critical images that illuminate the text. Grace Liu, from the Autodesk Intellectual Property team, was invaluable in completing all the necessary image permissions there.

My thinking about the current state of AI technology owes a debt to Mark Greaves of the Pacific Northwest National Laboratory, who has also contributed the Foreword. During autumn 2020 I often met Mark, Steve McConnell of NBBJ and the writer Cliff Pearson via Zoom. Our regular AI salons, as we called them, replete with just a splash of scotch, did much to clarify for me what can be the daunting trajectory of the development of intelligent machines.

Here at Yale today I came to rely on our able architectural librarian in the Hass Arts Library, Tess Colwell, without whom I would have been unable to navigate the university's vast, but often opaque, resources. Dean Deborah Berke has been unfailingly supportive as I laboured to complete the manuscript while we steered the School of Architecture through the global pandemic. And my editors at RIBA Publishing – Clare Holloway, Scarlet Furness, Liz Webster, Richard Blackburn and Ramona Lamport – are exemplars of professionalism and patience, particularly with my peripatetic schedule. Clare was not fazed a bit when I asked for my long-time friend and collaborator, the editor Andreas Müller, to pitch in as an additional set of eyes on the project. Andreas, who edited my last manuscript, offered regular, clear and very useful advice to improve both the flow and logic of the argument.

A final note of thanks to my partner Nancy Alexander, who always creates the space in which to do important work and the reminders for why it is so important to stick to it. Without her unending support, none of these projects would ever be possible.

FOREWORD

When I first started working with Phil, I held the one-dimensional impression of architecture that he mentions early in the book: architecture as a discipline that translates desire and capital into occupiable space. Although truthful and concise, this formulation makes it disturbingly easy for computer scientists like me to view architects as people who mechanically execute a semi-formal translation function. It took several Zoom-mediated and whiskey-lubricated discussions of architecture and AI for Phil and his patient colleagues to gently disabuse me of this blinkered and reductionist view.

The change in my own conception of architecture is not unlike the recent and dramatic evolution of AI, which is why this book is so timely for both of our professions. In the last decade, AI has rapidly advanced from meticulously authored rule systems to the staggeringly complex world of deep learning networks and self-supervised methods. Instead of relying on collections of intricate rules manually programmed for specific tasks, modern machine learning systems now base their outputs on impenetrably complex patterns that result from automatically analysing massive data sets. AI-generated design, which was once mostly an academic exercise in combining rules in different ways, can now produce creations that are far more subtle and compelling.

The need to reflect on architecture in the age of AI is therefore much more acute than it was even five years ago. Although machine learning will not make professional architects obsolete, neither will it have zero impact. The combination of Phil's deep knowledge of the architectural profession and substantial AI chops allows him to investigate the space between these two extremes and explore how modern AI can affect the intricate information structures that underlie the delivery of a constructed building. Phil also grapples with the elephant in the room: can AI ever adequately comprehend the deeply human context of places, replicate the architect's unique blend of formalism and creativity, and be responsible for the safety and fitness of a building? To address this, Phil's analysis goes beyond the usual reductionist critique and considers how modern AI could not only make the overall value chain of architecture faster or more efficient, but also result in a stronger architectural profession overall. I find this book tremendously thought-provoking, and I hope you do as well.

Mark Greaves, Mercer Island, WA

INTRODUCTION

Almost half a century ago I was an undergraduate-aspiring-architect studying at a school where the design studio was reserved for the elders while the rest of us fulfilled our general requirements. An early interest in computers had led me to a lower-level course called 'Introduction to Computer Graphics', where, according to the syllabus, we were to spend the first three drab weeks programming oscilloscopes to draw circles; exercises in early computer-aided design (CAD) on the first graphic displays – which were, of course, about 6 in wide, as seen in Figure 0.1.

Deciding that slog was not for me, I stumbled upon an exotic class in the same department called 'Natural Language Processing', where, apparently, we were going to teach computers to understand English. Our avuncular – if prickly – professor, Roger Schank, explained that he had uncovered one of the fundamental aspects of human existence by discovering the structure of language understanding encoded within the mind. Our job was to translate that theory into computer code. Of course, we were doing so on a 16-bit predecessor of the IBM PC called a PDP-11/45, with a whopping 256 kilobytes of main memory. One afternoon, in the computer lab, with ten or more of us working on the system, it burst into flames.[1]

0.1:
A CATHODE RAY
OSCILLOSCOPE,
C. 1996, NOT
MUCH CHANGED
FROM ITS 1975
PREDECESSOR
(COURTESY
OF MAKEHAVEN
INC.)

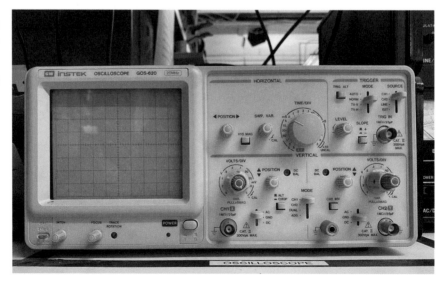

0.2:
AN EARLIER
VERSION OF
THE PDP-11
COMPUTER,
NOT ON FIRE[2]

My project for the semester was to write a program that would accept input from what was then called a 'newswire' – a text streaming service derived from teletype that delivered news from national sources – about the particular topic of oil tanker crashes and resulting spills, and then answer simple questions about the same. Our solutions essentially 'hard-coded' the extraction of meaning from English sentences and built semantic structures from which the machine could perform what we thought was inferential reasoning, all based on the thesis that we were digitising the thought processes also used by humans. My solution, while adequate, was no early version of Google. It also became clear by the end of the term that my days in the computer science department were numbered, as the professor correctly observed that my particular solution could not differentiate between a tanker accident and a car crash. I beat a rapid retreat to the entirely analogue architecture curriculum the next semester.

Like my early academic experience, architects have always had an ambivalent relationship with computation. In the early days of computer-aided design, we worried that the ancient art of drawing would be lost.[3] As the industry transitioned in the 2010s to 3D digital representation, and particularly building information modelling (BIM), anxieties increased that tools would diminish the designer's authorial agency when digital building components became standardised and dispensed with ease into our designs by increasingly powerful tools. Now that computation has become ubiquitous and machines are learning to perform knowledge work through artificial intelligence, the profession believes itself once again under threat. While the University of Oxford's Richard and Daniel Susskind, exploring the implications of artificial intelligence on the work of professionals, have suggested that 'we will neither need nor want professionals to work in the way that they did in the twentieth century and before',[4] there is very little computational intelligence impinging on the practice of architecture today. Yet we worry. Are we headed to a world where computers largely replace architects altogether? Surely there are reasons that this will not be the case?

Here is one example. When computers design buildings, the public will lose out. *Why? Because when an architect imagines a building, it is from its base upwards. What you see is an imagined image of what is being created from bottom to top. A real building shows us a holistic structure that starts from the very foundations and works all the way to the top, from foundation to roof, and so on. If we do not know the foundations of the building, we do not know what we are being sold, and we will not understand what we are looking at. The bottom line is that there is little or no aesthetic value in a building that has no soul, and so the negative view of digital architecture is not justified.*

Why? Because when architect imagines a building, it is from its base upwards. What you see is an imagined image of what is being created from bottom to top. A real building shows us a holistic structure that starts from the very foundations and works all the way to the top, from roof to foundation and so on. If we don't know the foundations of the building, we don't know what we're being sold, and we won't understand what we're looking at. The bottom line is that there is little or no aesthetic value in a building that has no soul and so the negative view of digital architecture is not justified.

I see two reasons why digital architecture is lacking aesthetics. First, it is solely a technical process. If you try to make the process of creating a building into something beautiful, a lot of work will go into that, and you won't save much in time. And second, digital architecture uses software as the sole element in the building process, which we know is unreliable. Software is so far from being easy to understand, we wouldn't even recognise it as software. We can't see a word of the message it's trying to send. So, it's not easy to tell from looking at a building whether it was designed by a computer or not. The work of design is not something we can simply throw into the computer and have it turn out like a BMW.

Digital architects try to make the process of creating buildings into something beautiful, but ultimately they don't deliver. There are other issues with digital architecture. To make the building more "real", you need software to manipulate the material the building will be made from. In the past, materials were never digitally designed, so when a digital architect took the material out of a computer, the software had no idea how to work with it, and the result was a "coffin" with "free" space at the base. Digital architecture only takes you to the model first, and once it's built, it will only keep it in the model, and create something completely different with it. Digital architecture can give you better clarity, but at the cost of aesthetic. It has never produced anything that looks like a real building.

Here's hoping, dear reader, that you're still with me after that brief italicised diversion, which was generated entirely (and unedited by me) with a technology called GPT-3, the third generation of what is called a Generative Pre-Trained Transformer, an artificial intelligence (AI) system that conjures original text in response to a prompt, which in this case was '(w)hen computers design buildings, the public will lose out'.[5] GPT-3 is my oil tanker program run in reverse – instead of merely absorbing a narrative to somehow understand, it creates one. It runs on computers orders of magnitude more powerful that were programmed by much more talented people.

The sample output above has an uncanny similarity to coherent English, the broad framework of an 'original' argument and even cites concrete examples. It has the maddening quality of bare intelligibility, as the more you think you understand it, the more obscure it becomes. GPT-3 technology is the current generation of machine intelligence that 'learns' language by ingesting huge amounts of text from the internet and 'teaches' itself underlying semantic structures. This is the same strategy that the mostly reliable Google Translate uses to translate a web page from English to Spanish, but greatly accelerated by rapidly advancing machine learning (ML). Yet both my early effort and that of GPT-3, above, lack real coherence, and the more time spent reading the text above, the less sense it seems to make. GPT-3 is certainly a more efficient approach than mine of 1976, but without the sweeping philosophical assertions.

Yet, the possibilities here are intriguing. Could a computer design an entire building well? The computer scientist, Mark Greaves, who contributed the Foreword to this book, describes the advances in natural language generation with tools like GPT-3 as having 'fluency and expressivity':

>> *Using modern ML techniques, machines are starting to successfully perform creative, original tasks in domains like language that were once uniquely the realm of humans. There have certainly been limited achievements based on more traditional AI which have been called 'creative', such as the famous 'hand of God' move played by Deep Blue in its chess match against Garry Kasparov. But these are quite rare... These systems seem to exhibit a level of creativity and expressiveness and linguistic artistry that machines hadn't reached in the past. And, in the realm of game playing, ML-based AlphaGo has shown real creativity as well.[6]* <<*

Creativity and coherence do not equate with competence, however, and therein lies at least part of the answer to the question that this book will explore. To wit, how should the profession of architecture consider and respond to futures made possible by advances in artificial intelligence, the so-called 'Second Machine Age'?[7] Having moved deliberately, if reluctantly, through the eras of both CAD and BIM, can we propose a willful, designed route – a professional strategy – that acknowledges the inevitability of a preponderance of intelligent machines in every dimension of design, construction and built asset operation while maintaining a proper role for human architects?

This is not a new question, at least as far as the relationship of machine intelligence and its implication for Design with a capital D is concerned – always the first place that architectural theory visits when struggling with a big problem.[8] Unexamined, however, are the implications for the practice, rather than the result, of architecture. If designers solve, as described by Peter Rowe (quoting Horst Rittel) 'wicked problems',[9] with open-ended beginnings and no fixed conclusion, competent practice requires heuristics across a broad spectrum of technical and aesthetic issues. This would seem to be a strategy that is exclusively human. However, computers are increasingly able, empowered by machine learning, to learn these techniques, and when they do so, professional strategies and methods – and the value of designers themselves – will be inalterably transfigured.

For the practice of architecture, the implications of this change are nascent. Machine learning algorithms are evaluating mortgage applications, reading routine X-rays, inventing never-before-seen strategies for playing board games, and even getting dangerously close to composing coherent ideas. However, AI-based approaches to the design generation are only now becoming apparent and none are commercially viable. As Daniel Susskind predicts in his second book, computers are increasingly becoming capable of tasks, as opposed to entire jobs.[10] Across the spectrum of services that architects provide, there are ample opportunities for the automation of tasks. Does that mean architectural work will be replaced, or by contrast augmented, by capable computers? Rather than wrestle with the larger question of whether we are to be wholly replaced by machines, perhaps a more intelligent route can be found where computers assist in the critical, but more mundane, aspects of practice: those that drive project delivery, technical precision and performative predictability.

At this juncture, the architecture profession itself is not under existential threat, but neither has it developed a strategy for the inevitable advent of learning machines. That strategy should have an expanded remit beyond our usual worries about our agency as designers and look more broadly at how powerful computation may affect our roles in the formulation, conception, delivery and use of buildings, and thereby the essential value of the profession of architecture itself. To that end, this text will examine three aspects of practice in the upcoming age of computer intelligence that in combination give us a view towards our fate:

1. How the **processes** and methods of practice may change.
2. What those changes will mean for our **relationships** to the systems of delivery in the built environment.
3. What opportunities there may be to refactor and improve the **results** of our efforts.

In concert it will attempt to propose a strategy for the profession going forward into the age of machine intelligence.

FRONT MATERIALS

PROCESS

ARCHITECTURE IN THE AGE OF MACHINE INTELLIGENCE

RELATIONSHIPS

Understanding the implications of a disruptive tool like artificial intelligence means exploring the relationship between the enabling **technology**, the **agency** of architects in deploying that tool towards new ends, how that agency might change the architect's role in the systems of project **delivery**, and finally how the **value** of the architect's services might change accordingly. Each of the following chapters is a different take on the combination of these questions.

RESULTS

CONCLUSION

END MATERIALS

TECHNOLOGY
AGENCY
DELIVERY
VALUE

01
PROCESS

>> HOW WILL THE PROCESSES AND
METHODOLOGIES OF ARCHITECTURAL WORK
CHANGE UNDER THE PRESSURES (AND
POSSIBILITIES) OF INTENSIVE AUTOMATION?
WHERE IS OUR WORK BEST AUGMENTED OR
INEVITABLY SUPPLANTED? <<

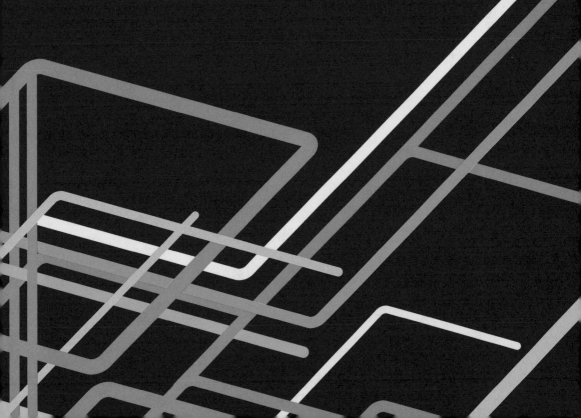

1.1
TOOLS AND TECHNOLOGIES

>> COMPUTERS HAVE BEEN DEPLOYED OVER
THE LAST TWO DECADES LARGELY IN THE
SERVICE OF MORE EFFICIENT DEPICTION AND
REPRESENTATION. ARTIFICIAL INTELLIGENCE
SHIFTS THE FOCUS FROM REPRESENTING A
DESIGN TO REASONING ABOUT IT DIGITALLY
— IN SOME CASES WITHOUT THE NEED FOR
A HUMAN OPERATOR OR EVEN MUCH HUMAN
INTERVENTION. WHAT DOES THIS MEAN
FOR THE EVOLUTION OF THE INSTRUMENTS
AVAILABLE TO MAKE ARCHITECTURE? <<

TAXONOMY OF TECHNOLOGIES

Various scholars have written the history of technology in the architecture profession and it is beyond the remit of this project to reprise that history in detail here.[1] It is possible, however, to see that history organised along two axes: the progression of technologies that comprise the toolkits of architecture, and the taxonomy of uses these tools support. Artificial intelligence – defined broadly as the ability to perform complex cognitive tasks in ways that produce results akin to the human mind – is an enabler of the various tools described in this taxonomy.

On the first axis, a vast simplification of the history of technologies in our discipline could start as far back as 2150 BC, with a statue of the Mesopotamian ruler, Gudea, that depicts a drawing of an architectural plan sitting on his lap,[2] marking the putatively first evidence of analogue drawing of a design. For at least the next 42 centuries architects abstracted their ideas by depicting design, explicitly or implicitly at scale, on pieces of paper. Mario Carpo maps this process in digital terms by suggesting that drawings and allographic notations, as vectors of design information, are actually a way of processing data with the very limited 'central processing unit (CPU) cycles' made available by manual graphics.[3] With minimal expenditure of energy – the act of drawing two parallel lines on a piece of paper – the architect could imply the construction of a three-dimensional, tectonic, materialised wall in the actualised building, and memorialise that rich idea for reference by the entire enterprise responsible for making it.

1.1.1: GUDEA, WITH A PLAN DRAWING IN HIS LAP, *C.* 2150 BC[4]

COMPUTER-AIDED DESIGN

In the penultimate decade of the 20th century, architects moved in earnest into their first foray of digital, computer-aided design (CAD, sometimes referred to as computer-aided drafting), whereby the mechanical process of inscribing lines, arcs and circles on paper was replaced by creating those same lines on to a virtual plane by inputting digital lines. While the vast investment in computers and plotters made this transition feel monumental, it was in fact more of a translation of existing techniques of drafting into virtual form, the object of which was still the production of drawings – but more precise. The evolution of technologies of large-scale printing devices (like plotters) moved in parallel with the electronic drafting tools (like AutoCAD©).

The move to computerised drawing, while ushering in an era of curvier buildings that were suddenly easier to draw – and to a lesser extent also easier to build – by virtue of the more precise geometry afforded by CAD, did little to address the informational gap between the definition of a design, its intent by the architect and the builder's ultimate responsibility for its construction, a divide defined in the Renaissance by Alberti in *De re aedificatoria*.[5] According to Carpo, Alberti set out the proposition that architects draw and builders follow those drawings without deviation. CAD gave architects an opportunity to draw faster, with more graphic consistency, and even reuse certain representations (like AutoCAD© blocks) across multiple sheets of a drawing set or even multiple projects. Yet, despite the added informational power of this data, the quality of work itself did not improve:

> *>> In short, the ontological gap between design intentions, their notation through construction drawings, and their material implementation leaves an inevitable grey area of undecidability, argument, frustration, litigation, and liability where all kinds of ad-hoc personal interventions, approximations, improvisation, bullying, persuasion, implorations, machinations, and subterfuge take the place of construction drawings and specifications, and haggling becomes the design instrument of choice.[6] <<*

Into this gap, 20 or so years later, came the next leap in representational technologies: building information modelling (BIM). In theory, BIM represented a flip of the traditional allographic strategy for architects: a 3D representation of the building was constructed in virtual digital space, from which those venerable drawings would be extracted as 'reports'. Gudea's floor

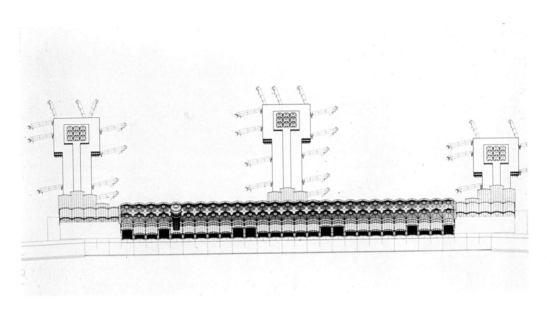

1.1.2: AN
EARLY CAD
DRAWING
BY PELLI
CLARKE PELLI
ARCHITECTS

plan, rather than representing the diagram of a design that otherwise lived in his head, would now be an extraction from full-scale digital replica living in computer memory – just another view of the relevant data. Every member of the design-to-build team could, in theory, add information to that model to complete their respective work. In practice, however, incompatibilities in process and outcome, the adversarial nature of building and the centuries-old allure of drawings have made BIM a tool used largely for production of even better working drawings than CAD. Its epistemological value as an organising principle for the informatics of building is almost completely ignored.

The last 10 years have seen explosive digitisation of many aspects of modern life, and design and construction have been no exception. Powered by the ubiquitous availability of the massive storage and CPU power of the cloud, and the ability to deliver those capabilities virtually anywhere through the internet, the architecture/engineering/construction/operation (AECO) industry is adopting a variety of computational tools, if peripatetically.

Designers have an array of
»   modelling
»   rendering
»   data management
»   analytical platforms.

Builders, armed with digital tablets on the project site:
- » rely on digital versions of what used to be the exclusive domain of paper
- » use data tools to manage the array of administrative transactions that comprise the construction process, deploy drones and LiDAR (Light Detection and Ranging) to document construction progress.

Building owners:
- » demand digital documentation of completed projects in lieu of rolls of post-construction drawings
- » assemble data from sensor networks in their building control systems to optimise building performance.

THE DIGITAL INTERSTICE

All told, the AECO industry seems to have entered a 'computational interregnum' of sorts, where various processes across the delivery continuum are becoming digitised. As a result, the variety of programs, platforms, data types and supporting hardware is becoming as varied – and disorganised – as the disaggregated building industry itself. In 1970, Nicholas Negroponte anticipated this state when he suggested that any transition to computation first imitates directly the analogue process it proposes to replace.[7] As a result, we are likely to see more years of excitement and confusion as the building industry wills itself into its digital future at the same time that it gives up the simple 'interoperability' afforded by paper-based, analogue processes.[8] Desires for some sort of broad theory of global data exchange will remain strong, but unrequited, outstripped by a software market eager to address new opportunities and the inherent complexities of various processes that necessarily comprise the delivery chain.

The building industry is typically not well-enough organised, nor can it compile enough market clout, to adopt fresh technologies or innovations soon after their introduction. It often has to wait until hardware, software or business models are sufficiently mature for architects, engineers and builders to adopt, adapt and improve such systems for their use. Such was the case with CAD platforms, which were originated by the aerospace industry and had to be ported down to personal computers sufficiently inexpensive to be in reach of AECO customers. Similarly, modelling platforms such as BIM or high-resolution rendering eventually appropriated the tools of manufacturing and movie-making once those technologies were within economic reach.[9]

1.1.3:
A LIDAR SCAN
OF CONSTRUCTION
IN PROGRESS,
MAPPED AGAINST
A BIM DATA SET.
THE CONDUITS
(IN GREEN)
AND DUCTING
(IN BLUE)
ARE VIRTUAL
ADDITIONS TO
THE DIGITAL
SCAN FROM THE
MODEL.

MOVING TO MACHINE INTELLIGENCE

In an exception to this otherwise reliable rule of thumb, architects did lead
the charge with the earliest versions of machine-driven design: scripting. As
the first proponents of technologies, such as McNeel Grasshopper (and, later,
Autodesk Dynamo), architects defined and elaborated the idea of what is now
known as parametric, or generative, design, where computerised scripts drive
geometry engines (like Grasshopper controlling Rhino). However, after 20
years of such work, scripting capabilities are largely deployed in the service of
relatively minor problems, such as shape generation or fenestration geometry,
rather than systematic alternative generation or analytical evaluation. While
later-generation tools like Hypar[10] have begun to accelerate the idea of
generative design, the dearth of analytic tools to evaluate alternative designs
generated by scripting has generally limited their use to form generation.

Machine learning and artificial intelligence, the most recent tools on our
timeline, are likely to follow the typical path in order to reach architects.
While major corporations are already absorbing AI/ML capabilities into their
core operating strategies,[11] most artificial intelligence available to architects
is delivered through their smart phones, while we order dinner online or
request a ride to the office. A few promising start-ups and other experiments
are testing the technology on various tasks on the construction site (e.g.
worker safety checking through computer vision) or project administration
(e.g. managing vast swathes of change orders and requests for information),
suggesting that we are still in early days.

1.1.4:
AUTODESK
SPACEMAKER
AI'S
DESIGN AND
EVALUATION
INTERFACE

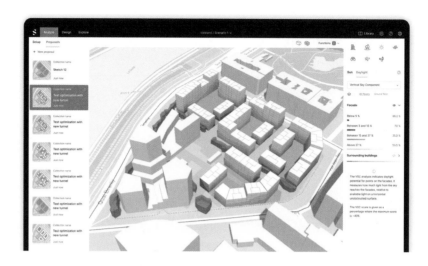

However, there are indications that this wait may not last much longer.
As I write this chapter in November 2020, Autodesk, my former employer,
announced the acquisition of Spacemaker, an AI-driven design generation tool
that evaluates site and building constraints and generates preliminary design
solutions (see Figure 1.1.4). That tool comprises a combination of design
representation, evaluative analysis and an AI infrastructure that learns best
results by interacting with its human decision-maker/operator.

As such, it may be an indicator of where the next generation of modelling
representation, beyond BIM, may be heading. The acquisition cost was $240
million, or 25% more (in 2002 USD) than the acquisition of Revit Technologies,
which started the BIM revolution in AECO in earnest.[12]

A TAXONOMY OF USE

In earlier work I have proposed a taxonomy by which the vast array of
digital tools emerging might be categorised, irrespective of their underlying
technologies.[13] In that analysis I suggest that the tasks of the building
enterprise, as supported by computation, fall broadly into four categories:

1. *Representation* (the depiction of authorial ideas).

2. *Analysis and simulations* (evaluation of those idea to understand their
    performance and implications).

3. *Realisation* (the translation of those ideas into built form).

4. *Collaboration* (the distribution and management of information across
    the enterprise).

As we consider the implications of machine learning and artificial intelligence in this context, those definitions require some additional refinement.

Representation

Drawings, text, images and physical models were the representational tools of the pre-digital age, followed by CAD and, eventually, BIM and parametric design. In a world of increasingly digitised data that might be consumed by smart machines, mathematical models and other data sets depicting a built asset – like sensor data coming from a building control system – should also be considered as representational. Further, as early forays into parametric/generative design suggest, algorithms that generate design are increasingly an important part of the representational process.

Analysis and Simulation

Computation is well-suited to examining data that results from representation in order to understand and evaluate it. Extended by the putative power of artificial intelligence, this capability might more accurately be described, as suggested by Agrawal, Gans and Goldfarb, as prediction: using (representational and other) data to evaluate the implications of design decisions and predict outcomes and implications of their underlying logic and decisions.[14]

Realisation

Design data is the logical underpinning of digitised construction processes. This is particularly true as construction, assisted by AI/ML, is automated and the processes of building are absorbed by machines that learn how to build. Those robots will need design data to guide them on the job site. Similarly, gathering information that documents the construction process – LiDAR scans of construction process that are mapped into BIM by intelligent systems are one example – is another aspect of digital project realisation.

Collaboration

From the early days of internet-based data management to today's common tools such as BIM 360, Procore or even Google Docs, project teams have needed to organise, transmit and manage digital assets irrespective of format. As we transit the digital interregnum, however, there is an increasing need to index, locate and understand all this data, much in the same way that modern search engines find information without user concern about format or location. Over time, digital design and construction will demand federated

	TIME	REPRESENTATION	SIMULATION AND PREDICTION	REALISATION	COLLABORATION
ANALOGUE	2500 BC – 1985	DRAWING AND PHYSICAL MODELS	EXPERIENCE, INTUITION, JUDGEMENT	MANUAL DOCUMENTATION AND ASSEMBLY	COLLECTIONS OF PHYSICAL OBJECTS
CAD	1985 – 2008	DIGITAL DRAWINGS VIA AUTOCAD©, RHINO	SCRIPTS, SPREADSHEETS	PHOTOGRAMMETRY, GEOMETRY-DRIVEN FABRICATION	COMPUTER FILES, OVERNIGHT EXPRESS
BIM	2008…	BEHAVIOURAL MODELS PARAMETRICS	BESPOKE ANALYSIS SOFTWARE	LASER SCANNING, DATA-DRIVEN MANUFACTURING	FILE SERVERS, CLOUD STORAGE SYSTEMS
DATA INTERREGNUM	2020…	AN EXPLOSION OF FORMATS	AN EXPLOSION OF TOOLS	DIGITAL INDUSTRIALISED CONSTRUCTION	SINGLE DATA ENVIRONMENTS
INTELLIGENT MACHINES	2025…	DATA LAKES	MACHINE- GENERATION PROJECTIONS	REAL-TIME DATA FEEDS, ROBOTICS	MACHINE-GUIDED INTEROPERABILITY

1.1.5:
RELATIONSHIP
OF
TECHNOLOGIES
AND TOOLS
OVER TIME
project informatics across the enterprise, where data structures in differing formats are connected to form a coherent whole with distinct parts. It is highly unlikely that standard data formats or interoperability protocols will allow all this data to become useful across the varied processes of construction. Machine learning algorithms may well be our only strategy to make sense of it.

THE EVOLUTION OF TECHNOLOGIES AND TOOLS

Each of the technologies described above – analogue drawing, CAD, BIM, and ultimately AI/ML – will change the way work is done and the tools deployed to accomplish it. The intersection of technology types and the evolution of the resulting processes and procedures they enable is described in Figure 1.1.5.

Computational power, reliance on automation, depth and breadth of data resolution and precision increase dramatically as our profession has moved from the upper left to the lower right on this grid. Certain aspects of design autonomy will be refactored as machines take over some – but not all – of the tasks of the architect. Figure 1.1.6 describes some of these possibilities, mapping the evolution of our four categories of technologies against both the data richness of the design enterprise (the top curve) and the automation of design process (the bottom curve).

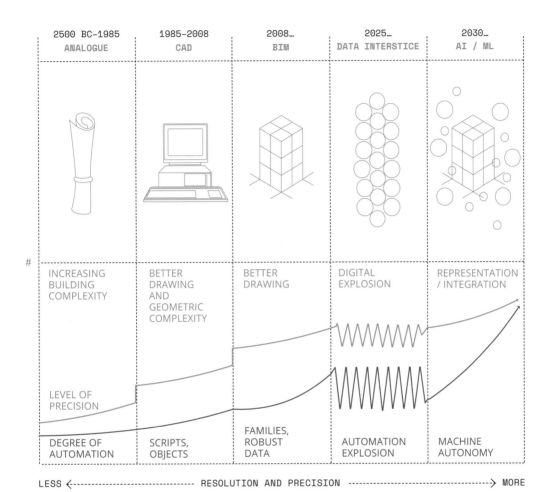

| 2500 BC–1985 | 1985–2008 | 2008… | 2025… | 2030… |
| ANALOGUE | CAD | BIM | DATA INTERSTICE | AI / ML |

\#

INCREASING BUILDING COMPLEXITY

BETTER DRAWING AND GEOMETRIC COMPLEXITY

BETTER DRAWING

DIGITAL EXPLOSION

REPRESENTATION / INTEGRATION

LEVEL OF PRECISION

FAMILIES, ROBUST DATA

DEGREE OF AUTOMATION

SCRIPTS, OBJECTS

AUTOMATION EXPLOSION

MACHINE AUTONOMY

LESS ←-------------------------- RESOLUTION AND PRECISION -------------------------→ MORE

▬ DESIGN REPRESENTATION
▬ DEGREES OF AUTOMATION

1.1.6:
HUMAN *VS*
MACHINE
AUTOMATION

It is suggested here that as tools become more enabled, there are parallel increases in the granularity and complexity of resulting information, along with the potential, in the digital era, for computational automation. During the drawing era, for example, informational complexity increased only with a similar change in the technical demands of construction itself, with the introduction of modern construction systems and complex delivery models. Automation was not available at all. The advent of CAD allowed for additional geometric complexity, more extensive documentation (in theory) and some automation through standard component libraries and scripting tools inside the CAD programs themselves, such as AutoLISP in early AutoCAD©. Those early scripting tools allowed the functions of AutoCAD© to be recorded and repeated; their successors in Rhino controlled dimensional parameters of the geometry model and gave the designer an ability to generate new forms.

A significant jump on both curves is apparent with the advent of BIM, however, as representation switched from the abstraction of drawing to virtual 3D models in parallel with parametric BIM families and data sets, and generative design approaches through mature scripting that will memorialise processes and procedures once dependent on human intervention. While scripts within CAD simply manipulated geometry, tools like Dynamo allow a designer to parametrically manipulate both the components of the design (like the size of windows) and their relationship to the overall building (like the location of the windows within an exterior wall). In the interregnum, we will see extensive generation of digital data and the episodic automation of various processes that would be otherwise disconnected.

The transition to broad-scale AI/ML will greatly enhance both the amount and the value of its precedent digital sources, serving as data lakes for intelligent machines to learn from. At the same time, computers will start to train themselves to perform machine-automated tasks. Those same machines will teach themselves about the relationships of the heterogenous data sets that comprise projects and create an 'interoperable' constellation of AECO data.

These trends portend a potentially daunting – but entirely necessary – trajectory for practice as the complexity of buildings and the power of computers advance in parallel. In combination, sophisticated digital modelling enhanced by machine intelligence will likely draw together the disparate forces of design, construction and building operation in a single, consolidated effort, coalescing around the data about the enterprise of building, from inception to demolition. As Carpo speculates:

>> *Given the unprecedented power of digital simulations, one may surmise that at some point virtual models may become perfect duplicates of, and substitutes for, the buildings they represent – embodying and enacting all and every aspect of them. Their designers could then make a digital model just as builders would once have made an actual building, and the final translation from model to building would entail no intellectual (or informational) added value whatsoever.*[15] <<

The information about and knowledge necessary for building would, as a result, be dramatically transformed. But how?

1.2 WHAT IS ARTIFICIAL INTELLIGENCE (AI)?

>> THE IDEA THAT COMPUTERS MIGHT DRAMATICALLY AUGMENT THE CAPABILITIES OF HUMANS — OR POSSIBLY SUPPLANT US ALTOGETHER — IS MANY YEARS OLD. BEFORE SETTING OUT THE OPPORTUNITIES AND THREATS OF AI FOR ARCHITECTURAL PRACTICE, THIS CHAPTER WILL SKETCH A BRIEF HISTORY OF THE TECHNOLOGY AND POSIT A TAXONOMY BY WHICH ITS PRESENCE AND FUTURE MIGHT BE UNDERSTOOD AND PREDICTED. <<

ORIGINS OF GOOD OLD-FASHIONED AI

The computer scientist John McCarthy is generally credited with coining the term 'artificial intelligence' in 1956, suggesting that computing machines could somehow mimic the functions of the human brain. And long before computing was within reach of mainstream practising architects, Nicholas Negroponte and others were exploring the idea of digital design. As early as 1964, Walter Gropius acknowledged that there might be a role for these new machines in the profession, suggesting that 'it will certainly be up to us architects to make use of them intelligently as means of superior mechanical control which might provide us with ever-greater freedom for the creative process of design'.[1]

In 1958, the psychologist Frank Rosenblatt put forth a theory of 'perceptrons' that was the precursor of today's modern neural networks. Rosenblatt posited that it was theoretically possible to represent visual information by 'teaching' a crude digital facsimile of a human neuron, and thereby encode human knowledge in accessible form. A decade later, the theory was challenged by MIT's Marvin Minsky, who suggested that 'deeper' models (with more layers of such neurons) would never yield reliable results, presaging an argument in AI strategy that survives, in part, to this day.

1.2.1:
NICHOLAS
NEGROPONTE'S
URBAN 5
SEEK, BY THE
ARCHITECTURE
MACHINE
GROUP, AS
EXHIBITED AT
THE JEWISH
MUSEUM, NEW
YORK, 1970

At the same time Nicholas Negroponte was exploring more practical questions in his MIT lab, 'The Architecture Machine'. An architect by training, Negroponte experimented widely in the early uses of technology and design, anticipating our use of tools like large screens, video and cameras, machine intelligence and immersive environments. His efforts anticipated early strategies for artificial intelligence, positing the possibilities of 'an intelligent environment that we would all eventually inhabit and that would eventually surround all of us'.[2]

While Negroponte examined questions of the representation, generation and manipulation of 3D space, other work considered core to understanding human thought probed what was called natural language processing: computers understanding and creating the written word.[3] Computer scientists attempted to translate emergent theories of human cognition into software, creating computational and semantic structures to extract understanding from text and reason inferentially from that resulting knowledge. This established what has since been called 'GOFAI' or 'Good Old Fashioned AI',[4] as attempts were made to build models of human cognition.

By the mid-1980s, AI research and software companies were attempting to extrapolate these theories into commercial 'expert systems', in which the knowledge of particular domains were painstakingly encoded by human programmers into algorithms in order to transfer detailed domain knowledge into a computer that could, theoretically, replace its human counterpart. These efforts rapidly hit the limits of both the efficacy of theory and the processing and storage capacity of hardware. The 'AI Winter' ensued, in which attention (and funding) waned for many years and the promises of AI would seem unfulfilled.[5]

BEYOND PERCEPTRONS

By the 1990s, computers were getting faster, cheaper and more available, and a different strategy for AI emerged: neural networks and machine learning. Benefiting from the vast computing power – and equally gigantic storage capacities – of the cloud, AI systems began to be based on a digital emulation of human memory, encoding information and relationships in increasingly complex layers that could be indexed and accessed like hyper-intelligent databases.[6] The power of computation revived the theory of the perceptron. The definition of an expert system could shift from 'human-encoded understanding' to 'computer-generated expertise' through programs that 'learned' from examining enormous data sets. Machine learning programs could, by virtue of their ability to process vast amounts of example data,

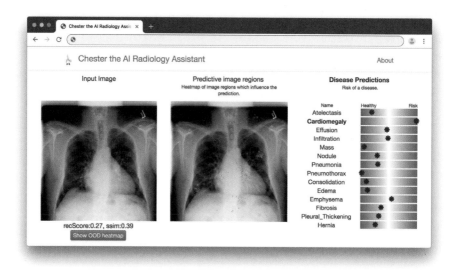

create statistical correlations that approximated learning.[8] Rather than somehow simulating the mechanics of human understanding, the goal of machine learning AI became software that could deeply learn – rather than be told about – the world.[9]

Nowadays, 'deep learning' comprises much of the academic and commercial work in AI and is often conflated with the broader definition of the term. Cloud computing infrastructure, fed by vast data sets coming from an array of internet-based sources, along with significant progress in the underlying learning algorithms, has brought AI into daily use, from smartphones to Google Translate. Computers are now world champion chess players, competent radiologists and credit scorers. Later generation ML programs can learn the rules of a game like backgammon by simply playing millions of simulated contests and testing what works best.

As capable as these systems appear, they do not actually understand anything, but have rather built semi-reliable statistical correlations of information relationships. In highly constrained contexts (where, for example, there is a well-defined training set, such as a game or a set of specific images), ML systems are surprisingly effective, and particularly today in the realm of natural language, as Google Translate demonstrates. As a result, much of the work in AI/ML today pursues this empiricist strategy. What the AI/ML systems entirely lack, however, is a rudimentary understanding of how the world works or anything remotely resembling common sense.

There is scepticism that without such an understanding of context, AI systems cannot be truly useful or reliable, and therefore if they will challenge the existence of, say, architects. The psychologist and entrepreneur Gary Marcus concludes that these 'narrow intelligence' strategies are flawed:

>> *(I)t is a fallacy to suppose that what worked reasonably well for domains such as speech recognition and object labeling – which largely revolve around classification – will necessarily work reliably for language understanding and higher-level reasoning. A number of language benchmarks have been beaten, to be sure, but something profound is still missing. Current deep learning systems can learn endless correlations between arbitrary bits of information, but still go no further; they fail to represent the richness of the world, and lack even any understanding that an external world exists at all.[10]* <<

Marcus argues that the work should consider a return to the original motivations of the AI field – simulating human cognition – and combine the data collection and analysis capabilities of deep learning systems with new models of perception and inference. While some progress has been made on this front, such systems do not exist today and will depend on the digitisation of new theories of understanding and, particularly, causality.[11]

TOOLS OF INTELLIGENCE FOR ARCHITECTS

As AI becomes more capable, today's architect is presented with a range of potential sources of intelligence to deploy in the service of the craft:

- » her[12] own talents, skills and experience (as certified by, for example, their professional registration)
- » an array of hard-coded computer programs that achieve specific ends (such as energy analysis or structural engineering)
- » machine learning systems (which might learn from data coming from their design projects, or even sensors within finished buildings and provide insight), and
- » ultimately the speculative prospect of cognitive systems that can reason within context (only seen in science fiction today).

The latter three, based on technology, are summarised in Figure 1.2.3.

1.2.3:
COMPARISON
OF AI
TECHNOLOGICAL
TYPES

COMPUTATION TYPE	TECHNOLOGY	CAPABILITIES	EXAMPLE
ALGORITHMIC (TRADITIONAL SOFTWARE)	HARD-CODED PROCEDURES	AUTOMATION OF SPECIFIC PROCESSES AND DATA INTERACTIONS IN A HIGHLY CONSTRAINED CONTEXT	BUILDING INFORMATION MODELLING, ENERGY ANALYSIS SOFTWARE
EMPIRICIST (DEEP LEARNING AI SYSTEMS)	NEURAL NETWORKS	COLLECTION, CLASSIFICATION AND CORRELATION OF LARGE, HOMOGENOUS DATA SETS	LANGUAGE TRANSLATION, CREDIT RISK ASSESSMENT, WINNING JEOPARDY, PLAYING SUPER-HUMAN CHESS
COGNITIVE ('COMMON SENSE' LEARNING SYSTEMS)	CAUSALITY MODELS AND INFERENCE ENGINES	COMMON SENSE KNOWLEDGE OF THE WORLD COMBINED WITH ENORMOUS DATA SOURCES FROM WHICH TO REASON AND INFER	MEDICAL DATA QUERIES, TERRORISM, KNOWLEDGE DATABASES[13]

The computers available to architects today are more adept at direct problem-solving than what Stanford Anderson once called 'problem-worrying', resolving the goals of the problem while simultaneously creating the design,[14] evocative of both Negroponte's and Peter Rowe's interest in heuristics as a strategy for solving 'wicked problems'.[15] Hard-coded software single-mindedly solves specific problems; your cost-estimating system will tell you nothing about the fire exiting required of your design, nor is it capable of learning how to do so. Emerging AI/ML systems, now being applied to problems of the built environment, may be able to evaluate or even predict issues in a specific context, but certainly are nowhere near ready to design entire buildings, heuristically or otherwise.[16] And, as of this writing, devotees of cognitive systems have spent decades building 'real world knowledge' as the basis of a next generation inference system, with limited success.[17]

While questions of human consciousness are not considered here, it is fair to describe intelligence – artificial or otherwise – as the ability to amass, organise and reason inferentially about heterogeneous collections of knowledge in context. Marcus believes this robustness cannot be currently achieved by today's AI systems, which are unable to 'reason flexibly and dynamically about the world, transferring what is learned in one context to another, in the way that we would expect of an ordinary adult'.[18] The work of architects surely qualifies as 'higher-level reasoning' in Marcus's terms, as he suggests that 'where there is no coherent, causal understanding of basic concepts, there may be no way to engineer robustness in complex real-world environments'.[19]

Early attempts, however, are beginning to emerge, with Autodesk's Spacemaker AI acquisition as a primary example. That tool uses a combination of modelling, analytical algorithms and AI to generate and evaluate planning alternatives, and then 'learns' about best practice by compiling results garnered from both the result of analysis and the choices of the human designers selecting the best options.

MACHINE CAPABILITIES

AI expert Mark Greaves describes the capabilities of current AI systems within a continuum from evaluation (understanding the implications of information), to simulation (using information to approximate similar circumstances in a different context), through to generation (creation of new ideas).[20] I will add to his categories, which are generally based on Bloom's Taxonomy of learning[21] (to which we will return later), a fourth, earlier capability of lesser profundity, 'understanding,' where the system can locate, access and deploy information.

Current capable empiricist AI/ML systems are excellent at evaluation (when systems read routine X-rays, for example) and even, in some circumstances, simulation (demonstrated best by extremely competent chess programs). However, examples of real generation, beyond the occasional flash of brilliance in the use of a hitherto never before seen Go move,[22] are limited, and there are no circumstances where computers are capable of generating a set of original ideas that comprise the design of something as complex as a building.

CAPABILITY	EXPLANATION
UNDERSTANDING	BEING ABLE TO FIND, INDEX, ACCESS AND DEPLOY DATA
EVALUATION	UNDERSTANDING THE IMPLICATIONS OF DATA BASED ON STATISTICAL ANALYSIS OF VERY LARGE DATA SETS
SIMULATION	PROJECTING FUTURE STATES OR CONDITIONS BASED ON CHARACTERISTICS OF PAST SITUATIONS OR CONSTELLATIONS OF DATA
GENERATION	CREATING ENTIRELY NEW IDEAS OR CONCEPTS BASED ON KNOWLEDGE AND UNDERSTANDING OF A GIVEN CONTEXT

1.2.4: MODIFIED GREAVES'S MODEL OF AI CAPABILITIES[23]

This is, however, only the current state of affairs and is a function of empiricist AI systems that can only 'deduce' based on massive correlations of data. It is likely that, over time, empiricism will give way to emulation of cognition as philosophers, neuroscientists, computer scientists and their commercial counterparts build ever more capable machines that move toward general AI, what Pedro Domingos has called the Master Algorithm,[24] in the service of what is now becoming known as 'artificial general intelligence', or machines that can both learn and reason about the world in context. Today, we are far away from such functionality, but it remains the grandest goal of AI development.

When Marcus's 'robustness' meets Greaves's generative capabilities, architects (and most of the labour force, as Daniel Susskind has suggested) have much to worry about, since '(q)uite simply, if we cannot count on our AI to behave reliably, we should not trust it'.[6] So, until then, the work of human architects is to orchestrate the combined tools of their talents, an array of software tools including BIM and emerging deep learning tools into coherent and valuable practice in anticipation of the day when cognitive platforms are readily available. By then, one hopes, the profession will have a firm grip on both the technologies available and the means to direct them.

1.3 PROFESSIONAL INFORMATION AND KNOWLEDGE

>> PROFESSIONAL KNOWLEDGE IN ARCHITECTURE IS AN INTRACTABLE CONSTRUCT, GIVEN THAT MUCH OF THE COMPETENCE AND DECISION-MAKING BY PROFESSIONAL ARCHITECTS IS BASED ON TRAINING, INSIGHT AND, MOST IMPORTANTLY, JUDGEMENT. TECHNICAL KNOWLEDGE IS NEITHER WELL-ORGANISED NOR EASILY REACHED. ASSUMING AI MAKES BOTH THE CAPABILITIES AND KNOWLEDGE BASE OF PROFESSIONALS MORE WIDELY ACCESSIBLE, PROFESSIONAL KNOWLEDGE WILL NO LONGER RESIDE EXCLUSIVELY IN THE MINDS OF HIGHLY TRAINED ARCHITECTS. DOES PROFESSIONAL DESIGN TRANSFORM? <<

PROFESSIONALS AND PROFESSIONALISM

In *The Future of the Professions*, Richard and Daniel Susskind's treatise on the potential demise of the professions in a world of increasingly capable artificial intelligence, you can find the following complete, if slightly tongue-in-cheek, definition of why society has created and empowered a class of professionals, architectural or otherwise (emphasis added):

>> *In acknowledgement of and in return for their expertise, experience and judgement, which they are expected to apply in delivering affordable, accessible and up-to-date, reassuring and reliable services, and on the understanding that they will curate and update their knowledge and methods, train their members, set and enforce standards for the quality of their work, and they will only admit appropriately qualified individuals into their ranks, and that they will always act honestly, in good faith, putting the interests of clients ahead of their own, we (society) place our trust in the professions in granting them exclusivity over a wide range of socially significant services and activities, by paying them a fair wage, by conferring upon them independence, autonomy, rights of self-determination, and by according them respect and status.[1] <<*

There is a social bargain defined here: running our world would seem to require both extraordinary expertise leavened by public trust, so we ennoble a small group of highly educated, certified and supposedly well-paid individuals to do very special things. Architecture, it seems, as the profession that translates desire and capital into occupiable space, falls under this rubric. And while some have suggested that this power and influence has failed the public it is intended to serve,[2] architects remain a crucial, if challenged, component of the equally challenged building industry ecosystem. That system, explored more thoroughly in Chapter 1.6, is largely organised in the service of making products – to wit, buildings and other physical infrastructure – yet architects as professional players within it have a distinctly different role: individuals with expertise who provide judgement and take personal responsibility for results of that judgement. In the systems of building delivery, this means that, unlike almost everyone else (builders, subcontractors, product suppliers, fabricators), professional architects provide services, not things. And as a result, they take personal, rather than corporate, responsibility for their actions.

The philosopher Donald Schön, who studied how professionals learn and deploy expertise, has suggested that architects and other professionals work in a way that is distinct from less institutionalised careers by virtue of what he calls 'reflective practice', or the ability to apply insight and make decisions through the implicit understanding gained with 'extraordinary knowledge in matters of human importance'.[3] What Schön called tacit 'knowing in place' we might call intuition, or the heuristic approach that Rittel describes as necessary to solve the 'wicked problems' of design.[4] We will examine later the question of whether an AI could even achieve such 'extraordinary knowledge', but for purposes of this specific exploration of professionalism, let us stipulate that the architect's synthetic role, by virtue of her professional responsibilities, is not well-replaced entirely by either empiricist AI of today or perhaps even tomorrow's cognitive systems that could somehow 'learn' all the procedures and processes of practice. If Schön is correct, there is something about professional knowledge that will lie beyond the reach of those systems.

However – and with AI, it seems there is always a 'however' – the formulation, design, procurement, construction and operation of a building is rife with procedural and data-driven tasks, ranging from calculating quantities to modulating temperature and humidity. As such, the systems within which those processes operate are sure to be influenced, if not partially transformed, by autonomous computing. The question for architects is where, how and what will tomorrow's AI-assisted architects really need to know?

WHAT IS PROFESSIONAL KNOWLEDGE?

In autumn 2020 I participated in an online panel of practitioners, educators and students to explore career prospects for graduates, during what we hoped was the latter stages of the global pandemic. Late in the discussion there was an exchange between the principal of a local firm and a well-respected, left-leaning dean of a New York school, comparing their respective expectations of professional know-how of recent graduates. Unsurprisingly, the practising architect wondered why his recent hires knew so little about 'how a building goes together' (a familiar refrain) or the processes or procedures of practice. The dean wondered why she should prepare graduates for a profession that currently seems so unsuited to the challenges – social, economic, environmental – of the times, and suggested that her job was to graduate students not in order to support the practice of today, but rather to radically reform it in and for the future. Unwilling to miss an opportunity to triangulate one of my favourite hobby horses, I asked the practitioner how the profession can simultaneously demand that graduates know so much more – and be delivered to them by the schools as 'mini-architects' – while paying them so little. The response was telling: in this local firm, reaching licensure meant a bump in pay of $1,000, or slightly less than 2% of what I expect he pays his least experienced staff.[5]

So, what do you need to know to be an architect? The vantage points of the panellists can be a good starting point: what do educators think a young architect needs to know to begin her career, versus the authors of professional licensing examinations and requirements? Of course, the timing does not correspond exactly, since licensure in the UK and US requires professional experience after education, but nevertheless a comparison of the two constructs is instructive. For purposes of this examination, I compare a curriculum with which I am deeply familiar (that of the Yale School of Architecture) and the post-graduate licensure competencies as outlined by the ARB Part 3 examination in the UK and the comparable standard in the United States: the Architectural Registration Exam (ARE) administered by the National Council of Architectural Registrations Boards (NCARB).[6]

At Yale, we require our 'Part 2' candidates (those getting a post-baccalaureate Master of Architecture degree) to be capable in the following curricular categories:[7]

> » **Architectural Design** – traditional studio pedagogy in the creation of a building design, focused primarily on the conceptual and schematic phases of the work.
> » **Visualisation** – depiction, through analogue and digital means, of ideas of building design.
> » **Environmental Systems** – the design and integration of structural, mechanical, electrical and other technical subsystems of building.
> » **History/Theory** – understanding the historical and theoretical platforms of the discipline of architecture.
> » **Building Technology** – seeing and performing the technical manifestation of building, including integration of complex systems, creation of construction documentation and field construction experience.
> » **Urban Design and Landscape** – understanding how buildings operate in the context of cities and sites.
> » **Professional Practice** – introduction to the profession, including ethical, legal, project management, business and project delivery aspects.

The comparable list of competency categories from the NCARB ARE is both more extensive and somewhat incompatible, with six major categories and almost 100 sub-competencies:[8]

» **Practice Management** – how do you run an architectural practice?

» **Project Management** – how do you manage, coordinate and lead a project through the stages of delivery?

» **Programming and Analysis** – how do you set up a project to be ready to design it?

» **Project Planning and Design** – what do you need to know to design a complete building that meets all applicable regulations and requirements?

» **Project Development and Documentation** – once the design is set, how do you properly detail, document and transmit that project to the builder?

» **Construction and Evaluation** – once the design is complete, how do you support and administrate construction, and evaluate the building after its completion?

The ARB, as a somewhat more parsimonious examiner, has fewer categories and only half as many sub-competencies (50):[9]

» **Professionalism** – how do you function ethically as a professional, and in a practice?

» **Clients, Users and Delivery of Services** – what is your role in organising, leading and managing a project?

» **Legal Framework and Processes** – what are the legal and regulatory frames of practice and building, and what is your responsibility for them?

» **Practice and Management** – how do you run an architectural business?

» **Building Procurement** – what are your roles and responsibilities during contactor procurements and subsequently, construction?

An informal mapping of sub-competencies against curricular categories yields an interesting disconnect, particularly as regards UK standards, suggested by the comparison in Figure 1.3.1.

It would seem that issues of practical implementation, and particularly as regards the business and processes of professional practice, are emphasised strongly by the ARB, and assuming that architecture curricula are generally

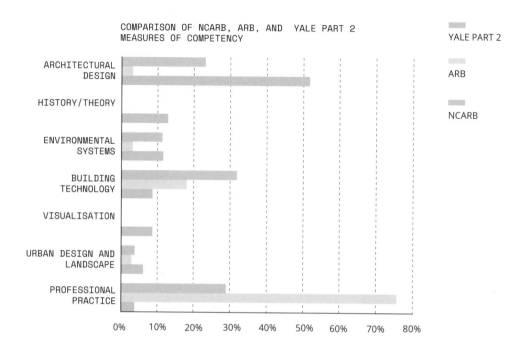

COMPARISON OF NCARB, ARB, AND YALE PART 2
MEASURES OF COMPETENCY

YALE PART 2

ARB

NCARB

ARCHITECTURAL DESIGN

HISTORY/THEORY

ENVIRONMENTAL SYSTEMS

BUILDING TECHNOLOGY

VISUALISATION

URBAN DESIGN AND LANDSCAPE

PROFESSIONAL PRACTICE

0%   10%   20%   30%   40%   50%   60%   70%   80%

1.3.1: COMPARING CURRICULUM AND COMPETENCIES, US AND UK FOR NCARB, ARB AND YALE PART 2

aligned around the world (having all been derived from a similar source in the Beaux Arts) there is generally a dramatic shift in emphasis as a student leaves the studios of schools and enters those of practice, with the resulting tensions illuminated during our panel.

An architect is trained on curricular platforms established by educators – and accreditors like ARB – to reflect an understanding of required aptitudes on the one hand, while professional licensing establishes a parallel, if different, level of minimal professional competence on the other.[10] As such, both are rough proxies for what our discipline believes an architect needs to know to practise. And while the American standard seems to emphasise the synthetic act of design itself in comparison to its British counterpart, an understanding of performance, practice and technical issues, as indicated by the emphasis on environmental systems, building technology and professional practice, appears to be, on the whole, a more important gauge of whether an educated student can be properly certified to protect the public's health, safety and welfare – the raison d'être for professional certification in the first place.

In a recent exploration of the implications of AI, the computer scientist Stuart Russell suggests that a fundamental characteristic of human reasoning, and with it, of human knowledge, is our ability to deploy our understanding in the service of actions hierarchically with 'dozens of levels of abstraction'.[11] He further invokes the Aristotelean concept of *practical reasoning*, the idea that knowledge and actions are rationally deployed in the service of achieving a specific goal.[12] For architects, those goals might be as limited as 'make sure this door swings in the right direction' to as lofty as 'try to stir the soul with this spatial experience'. The knowledge necessary to accomplish the former requires a rudimentary understanding of how doors work, perhaps in the context of a building regulation, while the latter likely demands the collective insight from a lifetime of work. Either way, each goal shares the common requirement that the architect reference proper, current and relevant information and apply her judgement in its use.

A talented designer deploys her skills in managing these 'dozens of levels of abstraction' in ways both poetic and technical, and much current work in architectural AI research, particularly in the academy, is focused on the former. Training machine-learning systems on thousands of beaux-arts floor plans in order to generate new options or using AI strategies to create novel aesthetic solutions is, of course, a valid avenue of exploration. It is not, however, the place where such systems are likely to have the most immediate nor important implications for practice in the near term and thus not the focus of the balance of this examination.

Developing a complete epistemology – aesthetic or technical – is a task for others, but for the purposes of this examination we might therefore conclude that architectural knowledge ranges from detailed technical information, through an understanding of procedures and processes, to insights gained from constant reapplication, refinement and synthesis during the course of career in the profession. Where might AI fit in to such a construct?

HOW MIGHT PROFESSIONAL KNOWLEDGE CHANGE UNDER AI?

The emphasis of licensing regulators on the more prosaic aspects of practice and professional competence would seem at odds with both the curricular emphasis of architectural knowledge as created in the academy and the need to train architects to face an uncertain future of new conditions, technologies and responsibilities.

1.3.2: AN
AI-GENERATED
IMAGE

It is not, however, incompatible with the current, or even immediately forthcoming, capabilities of artificial intelligence systems, which are very adept at collecting, indexing and referencing vast amounts of very 'thin' data. By 'thin', I mean epistemologically 'shallow' information: information that is largely devoid of machine-generated meaning or insight. Today's AI systems can absorb vast amounts of digital information, mostly words and images, but with scant real understanding of their underlying meaning or implications. Despite Mario Carpo's assertion that a completely digitally indexed world makes knowledge universally accessible and therefore the need for techniques like human reasoning or the scientific method obsolete,[13] we have yet to see machines with even the faintest idea of what a building actually 'is' – which will require the evolution of cognitive intelligence in order to usefully deploy the vast potential catalogue of building knowledge.

A brief demonstration tells this story well. Consider the image in Figure 1.3.2.

Two of today's supposedly 'best' AI capabilities are natural language processing and image indexing and generation. Researchers at the Allen Institute for AI, who work on understanding human implications of AI systems, have built a generator that creates images from its understanding of a short descriptive phrase. The picture here is the result of the phrase 'building in a city', not a difficult or particularly complex challenge. You can judge the result for yourself and try your hand at AI-created images on the Allen Institute website.[14]

Stipulating that computers in general, and AI in particular, are excellent at finding, sorting and cataloguing information and accessing it through correlation and statistics,[15] I would assert two related potential implications of the intersections of architecture, digital knowledge, and AI:

1. Most relevant – and certainly no surprise to architect readers – the world's architectural knowledge is dissipated, poorly organised and virtually inaccessible with ease. There is no architectural version of, say, the MEDLINE index, which cross-references all medical research, or (here in the United States) Lexus/Nexus, which provides access to the entire history of American legal cases. Proper medical treatment would be almost impossible without the former, nor could common law jurisprudence like in the US or UK progress without the latter.

2. Perhaps, therefore, the first role of any AI system aimed at the building industry could be getting our data, which are increasingly digitised and sorted.

1.3.3: LEXUS/ NEXUS LEGAL RESEARCH SYSTEM IN THE UNITED STATES. THERE IS NO COMPARABLE SYSTEM FOR ARCHITECTURAL DATA

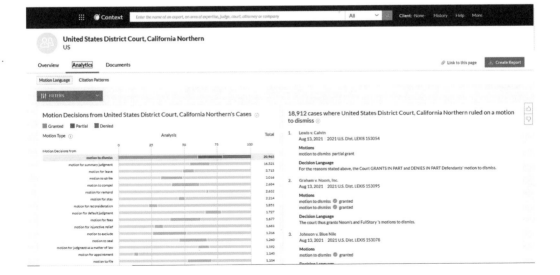

At the point where the numerous sources of architectural data, ranging from building product manufacturer's specifications to LIDAR scans of downtown sites in London, are accessible, next generation AI systems can not only begin to emerge, but proliferate to the point where both those systems and the data they catalogue can be of use. As I have asserted elsewhere,[16] measured performance based on data and analytics are likely to become a much more important part of design and construction as it digitises, and a first role of AI would be to help rationalise the informational platforms necessary to make that happen.

In doing so, one of the greatest yet untapped resources available to today's architects may become available to their successors, to wit, the digital project data, terabytes of which reside on servers in today's offices across the world, that are the artefacts of project work. As a practitioner in the 1980s and 1990s, despite all our digital drawings and other data, we relied on memory to inform us, with only our brains to connect our hard-won experience on previous projects with decisions we needed to make on our current jobs.[17] While today a human architect might have to scan a multitude of digital models to determine a best practice or trend illuminated by that data, an AI is well-suited to gathering and evaluating such information from a firm's archives.

1.3.4:
DIGITAL
INFORMATION
SOURCES AS
SUGGESTED BY
THE BUILDING
VENTURES
INNOVATION
NETWORK

MODELS	ROBOTS	VISION	METHODS	OTHER TECH	ENABLERS	
BIM	AUTONOMY	AR/VR	ADVANCED MATERIALS	ELECTRIC VEHICLES	AI/ML	IoT
DIGITAL TWINS	DRONES UAV	REALITY CAPTURE	MODULAR PREFAB	(TEX) TENANT EXPERIENCE	MOBILE	BLOCK CHAIN
GIS	ROBOTICS	COMPUTER VISION	3D PRINTING	BUILDING MANAGEMENT	COMPUTATIONAL	5G/LTE/Wifi

That same principle may apply to another intractable issue of architectural knowledge, the interoperability of information across digital systems. Figure 1.3.4 describes a potential array of today's digital information that could be rationalised by AI into new outputs. AI processes are well-suited to indexing, cross-referencing and correlating such data, and as such could become an implicit interoperability tool for AEC information, and thereby begin to build a more coherent informational platform for subsequent systems – disciplinary and computational – to evolve. A parallel concept in computer science, known as 'glue code', is a precedent. Glue code is comprised of computer instructions that operate at a low level in larger systems to connect disparate parts of a larger program, passing data from one subroutine to another. While hardly exotic, AI may be the glue code of architectural knowledge of the future.

NEW MODELS OF KNOWLEDGE

The broad outline of an argument to be built further in the balance of this text should be apparent: there is much to do and a long way to go before AI becomes even useful for architects, much less an existential threat. Let us assume that utility is preferable to destruction, that architectural processes (like many processes of the industry) are increasingly dependent upon computation, and that truly useful AI systems must rely on that data. There will likely be a time, perhaps a decade or more hence, where computational and epistemological coherence will combine for architects, and the days of disparate standards, incompatible digital processes and inaccessible insight will end.

That work will likely grow from the priorities of practice, which, as argued above, are largely concerned with the more practical, procedural and prosaic. And as other parts of the building delivery process, examples of which include feasibility studies, precision cost-modelling, construction automation and autonomous digital building operation, evolve through increasing digitisation, architects will need to understand how to manage and access information and deploy it in the service of the new responsibilities and professional obligations that will result. Where today's architect relies on passing familiarity with an ever-increasing pool of information combined with professional judgement and intuition, tomorrow's will likely need the intervening capabilities of AI to design.

1.4 AI AND PROCESS TRANSFORMATION IN DESIGN AND BEYOND

>> EMERGENT ARTIFICIAL INTELLIGENCE TECHNOLOGIES GENERATE AN ARRAY OF OPPORTUNITIES FOR DESIGNERS IN AN INCREASINGLY DIGITISED CONSTRUCTION INDUSTRY, WHILE SIMULTANEOUSLY INTRODUCING TREMENDOUS UNCERTAINTY IN DEFINING THEIR ROLES AND RESPONSIBILITIES. IN A WORLD OF ACCELERATED AUTOMATED PROCESSES, HOW MIGHT THE CURRENT TECHNOLOGIES AVAILABLE TO THE PROFESSION TRANSFORM AS AI BECOMES MORE CAPABLE? <<

My first real job in an architect's office was in the pre-digital era, long before computers became ubiquitous in the profession. The managing partner of our small practice in North Carolina returned to the studio one summer afternoon after a demonstration of a new technology called 'computer-aided drafting'. While he was deeply sceptical of the entire idea, and especially the cost, he noted that watching the plotter create a drawing was mesmerising, 'like a real draftsman[1] working on one part of the drawing and then another'. He also made it clear that no machine was going to be replacing anyone there laying down plastic lead on mylar sheets in our office in the foreseeable future.

My old boss was channelling architects' early but persistent uncertainty towards technology. While a decade earlier the visionary technologist Nicholas Negroponte and his colleagues were working at MIT on 'The Architecture Machine', mainstream practices like my employer were years away from anything more sophisticated than a word processing system.[2]

Somewhere in the space between Negroponte's research and my first drafting job tracing flashing details, one can find the dual anxieties at the heart of this ambivalence: the conviction that our work as architects is a uniquely valuable contribution, paired with the paranoia that capable machines will mercilessly replace us – the source of our profession's angst about machine intelligence and its putative disastrous effect on design process. However, as Stanford computer scientist, Roy Amara, is purported to have said, 'We tend

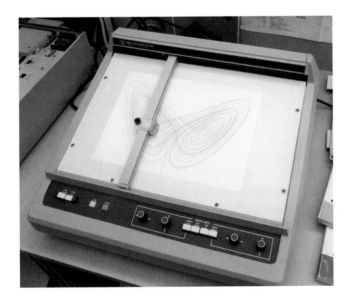

1.4.1: AN
EARLY PEN
PLOTTER,
C. 1980

to overestimate the effect of a technology in the short run and underestimate the effect in the long run,'[3] which is certainly the case with architecture's current concerns about artificial intelligence. The technological circumstances today are radically different from those of four decades ago, but the ambivalence justifiably remains.

Resulting concerns about the implications of AI on practice run the gamut from design theory to employment economics. Neil Leach wonders whether AI-enabled computers can be creative,[4] while Antoine Picon gingerly embraces the opportunities of machine-assisted design and simultaneously worries about AI restructuring the labour force:

>> *Until recently, one assumed that automation would impact only poorly qualified jobs. This might not be the case. Architecture will be probably among the most severely hit disciplines. The reason for this high degree of vulnerability is that architecture is among the most formalized of all the arts. The mechanical part is stronger than in other domains, and hence the traditional position of the discipline on the threshold between art and technology.[5] <<*

Labour economist Daniel Susskind (quoting the Governor of the Bank of England) refers to this phenomenon as 'the massacre of the Dilberts'[6] and challenges the value proposition of professionals more generally:

>> *(W)e argue that the professions will undergo two parallel sets of changes. The first will be dominated by automation. Traditional ways of working will be streamlined and optimized through the application of technology. The second will be dominated by innovation. Increasingly capable systems will transform the work of professionals, giving birth to new ways of sharing practical expertise. In the long run, this second future will prevail, and our professions will be dismantled incrementally.[7] <<*

There can be a wide gulf between theoretical speculation and the realities of daily practice, so now is an opportune time to bridge the two, lest the dismantling begin in earnest. Beyond theorising about the possibilities of this new technology – ignoring in the hope it will pass us by or fighting the inevitable automation of knowledge work – we should examine the relationship between design process and machine intelligence to determine how, if at all, they can at worst co-exist and at best be mutually complementary.

PROCESSES AND PLATFORMS

As the building industry has become increasingly digitised, an emergent taxonomy of data inputs, algorithmic processes and potential AI-assisted outputs is emerging. As the industry relies more and more on computers, it creates large pools of digital information. Those data are made accessible via so-called **common data environment** platforms that organise, index and reference the resulting information. They systematise both inputs and outputs created by the collection of current **automated process** tools common to the industry – CAD, BIM, analytical engines, spreadsheets and so forth. As AI tools become available to AECO, a new set of **autonomous process** tools will emerge that create results without the direct input and control that were necessary for their automated predecessors. The combination of all three process platforms – common data environments, automated process tools and autonomous processes – will generate a new series of potential **outcomes** that are likely to radically change design process and the architect's responsibility for results.

See Figure 1.4.1 for a diagram of these relationships.

1.4.2:
INPUTS,
PROCESS
TRANSFORMATION
AND OUTCOMES

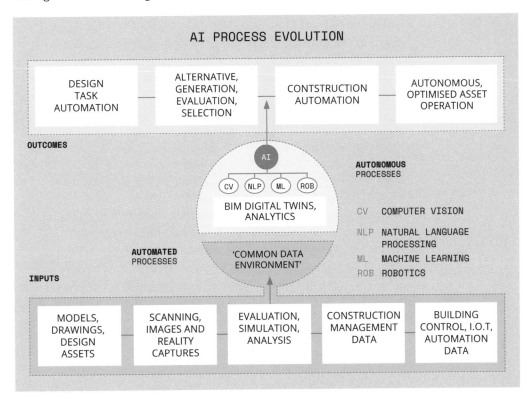

Today's building projects generate huge piles of digital information, as the tools of building are increasingly computer-based. While in the 1980s and early 1990s the most relevant digital output was created by either CAD or word processing tools (primarily by AutoCAD© and WordPerfect, respectively), some element of almost every part of the design-build-operate-use continuum is digitised today. The ease with which the architecture profession shifted entirely to remote work during the Covid pandemic demonstrates that design work can be largely digitised and is likely to remain so, permanently.

As we saw in the previous chapter, today's artificial intelligence systems, based largely on empiricist platforms, must consume vast amounts of digital information to reach some level of basic competence. Unfortunately, these data exist today in a wide variety of forms and formats, and are not nearly as heterogeneous as the records of thousands of games of chess or millions of pictures of cats.

However, it is possible to categorise digital building information in ways suggested by current practice and the likely evolution of digital techniques and processes, in order to develop intelligent input strategies for the futures of AI in design. Those categories include:

> **Design representations** in the form of models, drawings, studies, project management documents and other metadata generated as result of the creation of asset design, coordination and construction. Representational information is generated by the designers, builders and building operators to formally memorialise intent. Building information models (BIM) fall into this category and are important for other reasons that will be explored later.

> **Reality capture information** that documents existing physical reality, including topographic and GIS data, as well as video records, photographs (2D and 3D) and point cloud data from scans of existing conditions and construction in progress, all of which combine to translate the physical world of building into accessible, digital form.

> **Evaluation, simulation and analytical data**, including reference data sets that support design, engineering and construction management, analytical models for determining performance and simulations that use design representations as input to project behaviour of the project as it is being developed. Structural engineering analysis software, energy modelling and computational fluid dynamics models are good examples of what Andrew Witt calls 'technoscientific' models.[8]

1.4.3:
A BUILDING
INFORMATION
MODEL (BIM)

1.4.4:
A LIDAR
SCAN

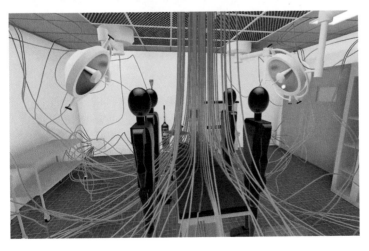

1.4.5:
DIGITAL
ANALYSIS AND
SIMULATION

1.4.6:
AUTODESK
B360
COST
MANAGEMENT
TRACKING
SYSTEM

1.4.7:
AUTODESK
TANDEM
DIGITAL TWIN

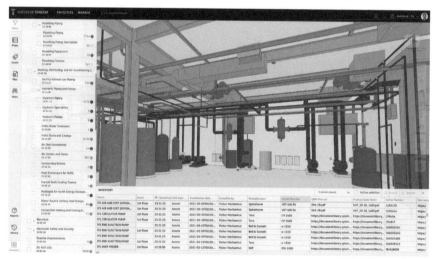

Control and coordination information generated by process control, monitoring and tracking protocols, such as construction management data systems, project control websites and cost estimating/management systems.

Asset operation, systems performance and use information generated from building management control systems and other sensors that run the asset, and internet of things (IoT) information depicting the interaction of users with the asset itself. As built assets contain more and more digital infrastructure of all sorts, the resulting data will accumulate as a record against which future designs can be developed.

In combination these data sources are incoherent, held together only by the abstract concept of 'the project' enterprise that originates, realises, operates and uses a built asset. Individually, however, they are well organised, indexed, consistent and thereby entirely accessible as data sources for machine intelligence systems, and in some cases may be generated by such systems themselves.

PROCESS TRANSFORMATION

At the centre of the transformation of data streams into new, digitally enabled outcomes are both existing and new software, platforms and computerised procedures that work in combination to move the work of architects to its digital future, comprised of three elements.

1. **Common Data Environment:** Streams of input coalesce in an environment called the Common Data Environment, or CDE, which is formally defined as 'agreed source of information for any given project or asset for collecting, managing and disseminating each information container through a managed process'.[9] That information structure creates an index referencing system for organising, locating, versioning and deploying various digital artefacts of the asset creation process (referred to above as 'containers') and as such provides referenceable 'containers' (using CDE terms) for the various input streams and data collections that accumulate during project asset creation.

The designers, builders and operators of a project then have two types of tools to either create or support their respective roles in the creation of a building: those that are 'automated' and those that are 'autonomous'. It is a distinction that will be important to define, during the balance of this book, how AI tools offer different opportunities – and threats – to the architect.

2. **Automated processes:** Automated tools are those digital instruments with which most architects are familiar today and fall directly in the category of 'algorithmic' machine intelligence. Any software tool today that, as an outcome of direct human manipulation of its capabilities, generates results and data based on a specific set of inputs could be characterised as 'automated'. For purposes of this discussion, we can use the example of BIM to illustrate this point.

An architect developing her design using a BIM tool is largely in complete control of the data creation process. She decides that her project needs doors, walls, windows and floors, and creates those elements digitally by instructing her BIM software to do so. Each of those elements has been algorithmically encoded to have specific characteristics; a door, for example, has a certain constrained relationship to a wall and in that sense has specific tectonic 'intelligence' that the architect deploys as she creates the model. The process of deploying that door is automated as she instantiates it into her BIM, and its representation in various modalities – the plans, elevations, sections, details, schedules – is automatically populated in those spots for her. Most traditional software tools available to the architect today are such 'automated' processes.

3. **Autonomous processes:** Artificial intelligence tools, however, are distinct from their automated counterparts in that they process and generate results without the direct intervention of the designer, operating autonomously. When our BIM-enabled architect above searches online for product information, for example, the search engine's AI-driven process combines what it has 'learned' as a machine about not just the realm of building product information on the web based on previous searches but what her specific interests might be, based on a model of her previous searches and its conclusions about the objectives she had in initiating the search in the first place. As such, the product search, and all such tools that today are based on AI/ML systems, are 'autonomous' and distinct from her BIM authoring experience.

A NEW GENERATION OF OUTCOMES

With increasingly large, better organised data sets accessible to AI-based systems, we can speculate on the likely set of autonomous opportunities that architects will see in the next decade as such systems become more capable and available. These categories, that we will call 'autonomous outputs' for now, form a speculative framework from which we can begin to build strategies for the implications for the profession, and might include the following:

Design task automation: Procedures and protocols that require the direct intervention of the designer as likely to be autonomous in the future. While most code checking is a manual process today, that procedure can be supported by submitting a digital model to a code-checking tool that uses AI to evaluate code compliance, combining a more traditional 'architectural' model with a technoscientific counterpart.

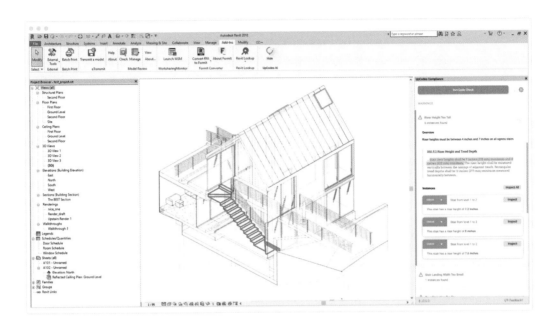

Tomorrow, that AI-based code checker could be lurking in the background of a BIM process, anticipating code-related problems as the designer creates her scheme. Similar autonomous protocols might reach across the entire delivery and operation life of a building.

1.4.8:
UPCODES
CODE-
CHECKING
SOFTWARE

Alternative generation, exploration: Design alternatives were once created entirely by direct manipulation of design information, like the cardboard models shown in Figure 1.4.9. Today this process is assisted by scripting, a form of 'automating' the control of certain digitally controlled parameters of a model to vary its characteristics and thereby create a variety of solutions. Those scripts are sometimes combined with analytical software – such as energy analysis – to evaluate and optimise the results. Scripts create the parameters by which designs might be generated in the future by AI.

Construction automation: As robotics accelerate with AI-assisted systems for control, enhanced by computer vision and bolstered by the advent of industrialised construction processes borrowed from manufacturing, construction tasks once performed exclusively by human workers will be augmented, and in some cases, replaced, by autonomous devices on the job site. An excellent recent example is the PictoBot, an AI-driven robot that works alongside an accompanying human supervisor to paint interior walls, otherwise unassisted. While the patterns, locations and finishes of such work might be specified in the architect's building information model, translating the designer's intent for a surface with those particular characteristics requires a context-dependent operation that can only mechanised effectively through some sort of computational intelligence.

Autonomous building function: If the architect's and engineer's initial BIM is a first functional descriptor of a building that might include the performance objectives of its systems (and the design of the control infrastructure that might implement that performance), the operating air, water, waste and signal systems of that building generate another digital collection of data that, in concert with real-time analytics, can be used to calibrate and optimise those systems. Companies that provide such building infrastructure, such as Johnson Controls, build not just, for example, an air distribution system but also the digital controls for the system that communicate with AI-based monitors that memorialise and optimise the system output and use of energy (thereby reducing carbon). Of course, the resulting analytical data sets, interpreted by AI, can also provide insight into the design of subsequent buildings and their component equipment.

1.4.9:
MANUALLY
CONSTRUCTED
STUDY
MODELS, C.
1993

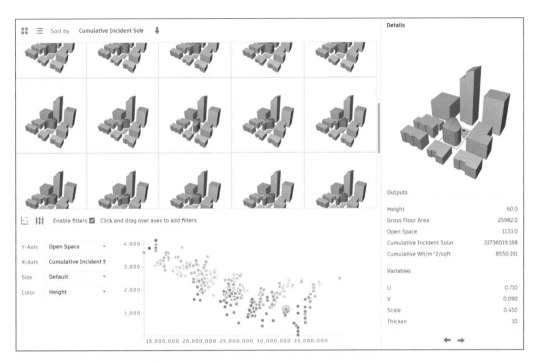

1.4.10:
SCRIPTING
TOOLS TO
GENERATE A
BUILDING
ENCLOSURE

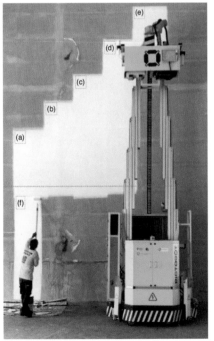

1.4.11
PICTOBOT, AN
AUTONOMOUS
PAINTING
ROBOT, AS
PROPOSED BY
E. ASADI, B.
LI AND I.
CHEN[10]

A VIRTUOUS LOOP

The relationship between today's largely automated processes used by designers and builders (like BIM) will, over time, give way to the autonomous opportunities of AI-based processes, and in doing so transform both the inputs and outputs of the building process. As computational platforms gain independence from their human masters, they themselves will generate additional sources of data in a potentially virtuous, self-reinforcing data loop. Properly guided, this cycle might bring the industry many of the advantages of productivity, efficiency and effectiveness that the designers, builders and users of buildings alike so desire. Doing so requires those same players to be directive about the generation of digital information and its intelligent use, with clear ideas of how AI might translate vast oceans of data into useful knowledge.

1.5 SCOPES OF SERVICE

>> DIGITISATION WILL CONTINUE TO
TRANSFORM THE WORK OF ARCHITECTS,
AUGMENTING AND SUPPORTING SOME
ACTIVITIES AND REPLACING OTHERS. WHILE
TODAY'S COMPUTERS DO SO IN A WAY THAT IS
LARGELY PROCEDURAL — ACCELERATING WORK
AND MANAGING COMPLEXITY — AI SYSTEMS
OFFER DIFFERENT OPPORTUNITIES AND
THREATS TO THE PROFESSION IN THE SCOPE,
BREADTH AND STRUCTURE OF THE SERVICES
THEY OFFER THE INDUSTRY. AS AI SYSTEMS
EVOLVE, SO WILL THEIR INTEGRATION TO THE
DAILY WORK OF ALL PROFESSIONALS AND,
EVENTUALLY, EVEN ARCHITECTS. <<

JOBS VERSUS TASKS

When Richard and Daniel Susskind argued in their 2015 book, *The Future of the Professions*, that artificial intelligence would eventually replace society's need for professionals, architects were understandably concerned. Ours is a precarious profession, smaller, less politically powerful and certainly less remunerated than our equally threatened brethren in law or medicine, who will certainly put up a bigger fight before allowing themselves to be automated out of existence. The Susskinds declared, right at the outset of their treatise, that

>> *... we are on the brink of a period of fundamental and irreversible change in the way that the expertise of specialists is made available in society. Technology will be the main driver of this change. And in the long run, we will neither need nor want professionals to work in the way that they did in the twentieth century and before.*[1] <<

They observed that society established professionals to dispense expertise, and in doing so those professionals horde expert information, control the access to it and deploy it in ways that can be easily automated by an intelligent machine. Radiologists will give way to algorithms who can more patiently and accurately read diagnostic images; attorneys will no longer be needed to search documents for evidence, prepare routine legal arrangements or even represent clients in disputes; and architects will not be needed to design, document or help build projects.[2]

As I write in 2021, we are six years past this declaration of extinction, with no significant encroachment by super-intelligent machines on the work of any of these disciplines. Best not get too comfortable, however, as technological change comes much more slowly to the building industry in general, and architecture in particular.[3]

The encroachment on architects and the services we provide is probably better described in Daniel Susskind's subsequent book, where he argues that it is likely that discrete tasks rather than entire jobs will be eliminated by computers. He extrapolates from the work of economists David Autor, Frank Levy and Richard Murnane, called the 'ALM hypothesis', drawing a distinction between entire jobs versus tasks, and routine versus non-routine tasks. Routine tasks (like many of those automated by mechanisation during the Industrial Revolution) require what ALM theory called 'explicit' knowledge, which is easy to document, explain and repeat. These are tasks based on 'implicit' knowledge – requiring, for example, the creativity and judgement of professional architects –

which will not be automated because it is impossible to capture such work with rules expressed with logical expressions such as algorithms.[4]

Susskind projects this thinking on to the current era of emergent AI to argue that machines may well encroach into the domains of implicit knowledge:

>> *The temptation is to say that because machines cannot reason like us, they will never exercise judgement; because they cannot think like us, they will never exercise creativity; because they cannot feel like us, they will never be empathetic. And all that may be right. But it fails to recognize that machines still might be able to carry out tasks that require empathy, judgement, or creativity when done by a human being – by doing them in some entirely other fashion.[5]* <<

Today's empiricist, deep-learning based systems are beginning to emulate creativity, but certainly not to the degree that, for example, one might be willing to entrust that algorithm to replace wholesale the professional judgement of an architect. In the meantime, it is more important to examine, through the lens of today's professional services, structures where AI might affect the tasks of professional work.

MACHINES LEARNING ARCHITECTURE

If today's most capable intelligent machines are based on various strategies for deep learning, we can evaluate their capabilities by what they can be trained to do. Mark Greaves's machine capability taxonomy, described in Chapter 1.2, was derived from a canonical reference known to many teachers, Bloom's Taxonomy of learning, which defines a hierarchy of capabilities that build from so-called 'lower order thinking' (like memorisation) to 'higher order thinking' (like creating something new). Bloom created this approach as a guide to choosing pedagogical strategies in the classroom, and his students, Anderson and Krathwohl, subsequently refined the hierarchy to the terms very familiar to teachers today,[6] and compiled in comparison in Table 1.5.1.

It can be argued that the most successful deep learning systems today – the ones that invent new game strategies and thereby annihilate their human opponents, credibly translate from English to Japanese or even compose music or paintings – have somehow climbed Bloom's pyramid, having gone far past remembering or even testing data to 'creating' new concepts. Within certain extremely limited contexts, like the specific rules of the game of Go, for example, or the 'learned' patterns of thousands of paintings, perhaps this is true. A machine programmed with a rigorous set of rules, however, can be

1.5.1:
LEARNING
TAXONOMIES

	BLOOM	ANDERSON/ KRATHWOHL	GREAVES	
HIGHER ORDER THINKING	CREATE	DESIGN FORMULATE DEVELOP		CREATE
	EVALUATE	DEFEND JUDGE SELECT		
	ANALYSE	COMPARE DISCRIMINATE TEST		SIMULATE
LOWER ORDER THINKING	APPLY	CHOOSE DEMONSTRATE SKETCH/SOLVE	EVALUATE	
	UNDERSTAND	CLASSIFY LOCATE TRANSLATE	UNDERSTAND	
	REMEMBER	DEFINE DUPLICATE MEMORISE		

said to have a ton of explicit knowledge, and as such is 'creating' in only a very limited way, particularly since the measures of success – winning the game or identifying a tumour on a radiograph – are so specific.

So let us assume, at least for the next few pages of this argument, that Susskind's thesis of task automation is the most likely implication of AI on architectural practice in the foreseeable future, and that selected tasks within the services that the profession provides may well be augmented, accelerated or even replaced by an intelligent computer. Susskind asserts that those tasks are easy to identify: they serve explicit goals that can be easily measured (to determine success) and there needs to be a lot of data for the machine to learn how to achieve the goal.[7] One might argue that a wide array of architectural tasks might fit this bill, including questions such as: 'Does this project meet the fire safety code?' or 'Does this ceiling plenum accommodate all the building services?' With enough data and proper training, could a computer achieve these goals? Or, even better, not just answer the question but generate the required design solutions to meet those needs?

Why not? That stuff either fits in the ceiling plenum or not, and those doors either have the right fire rating and swing in the correct direction, or they do not. Assuming our deep-learning AI could study enough ceilings and exit corridors, it should be able to learn right from wrong, and correct from negligent.

If only it were that simple, we could start building architectural intelligence into machines right away. However, there is another dimension to task automation, what Stuart Russell calls hierarchical planning and management:

>> *Intelligent behavior over long time scales requires the ability to plan and manage activity hierarchically, at multiple levels of abstraction – all the way from doing a PhD (one trillion actions) to a single motor control command sent to one finger as a part of typing a single character in the application cover letter.*[8] <<

In order to achieve specific goals, even those that require explicit knowledge and have clear, measurable outcomes, an intelligent machine must be able to deploy a hierarchy of (automated) tasks in an integrated order to reach that goal, and in doing so assure that the tasks work in concert towards the defined objective. Very few of the obligations of the architect today, even those reliant only on explicit knowledge, can be automated in this way, and as such it is unlikely that large swathes of design service will be satisfactorily automated in the near to middling future.

ARCHITECTURAL SERVICES

Modern architects deliver their services in a prototypical continuum that begins with project definition and extends through design to construction. In the UK, such services are well-defined by the RIBA Plan of Work,[9] and in the United States as 'Basic Services' by the AIA's Owner-Architect Agreement B101.[10] Each are compared in the diagram in Figure 1.5.2.

In general, each scope prescribes a route through a standard set of tasks that can be described in in categories like Project Definition, Design, Production and so forth. Each phase of the work is comprised of a series of subtasks that differ by phase and are modulated based on the expectations, deliverables and professional standards that govern the architect's services. These subtasks themselves can be categorised into general buckets like Practice Management, Project Management, etc, and they span across the phases of service. A rough mapping of a sample of such tasks, aligned with service categories, can be found in Figure 1.5.3.

STANDARD SCOPES OF SERVICE				
RIBA (UK)	**0** STRATEGIC DEFINITION	**1** PREPARATION + BRIEFING	**2** CONCEPT DESIGN	**3** SPATIAL COORDINATION
AIA (US)	**PD** PRELIMINARY DESIGN, PROGRAMMING		**SD** SCHEMATIC DESIGN	**DD** DESIGN DEVELOPMENT

SERVICE CATEGORIES				
DEFINITION				
DESIGN				
PRODUCTION				
PROCUREMENT				
CONSTRUCTION				
OPERATION				

1.5.2:
RIBA AND
AIA SCOPE OF
SERVICES

If we look at these task components through a lens that combines Susskind's 'clear goals and lots of data' criteria and Russell's task hierarchy, and includes the ALM's tasks that require implicit knowledge, we can start sorting the service work of architects by likelihood of empiricist automation.

Let us call any task component that can be easily defined with a measurable goal and executed through explicit logic as '**procedural**', those that require an intelligent integration of procedural tasks to reach a goal, even a measurable one, as '**integrative**' and those that are inherently creative, subjective and/ reliant on implicit knowledge as '**perceptive**'. Figure 1.5.3 attempts to categorise each component on this continuum, from procedural through integrative to perceptive, depending on the work necessary to complete each task component.

As the coded bars suggest, there is very little that today's architects do, even at this relatively detailed level of examination, that can be characterised as easily automatable. In fact, much of the technology of today is procedural (including every piece of software we use), all of which is deployed in the service of higher order tasks they accomplish. Eliminating humans from the architectural equation is going to require an enormous jump in capability, climbing the Bloom Taxonomy while combining those capabilities to accomplish hierarchically complex objectives. This suggests that architects would better

4 TECHNICAL DESIGN	NOT USED	5 MANUFACTURING + CONSTRUCTION	6 HANDOVER	7 USE
CD CONSTRUCTION DOCUMENTS	**PR** PROCUREMENT	**CA** CONSTRUCTION CONTRACT ADMIN	NOT USED	**POE** POST OCCUPANCY EVALUATION

spend time strategising which procedural aspects of practice might best benefit from autonomous processes of AI, rather than worrying that our work will be replaced wholesale by capable machines.

AI-SUPPORTING SERVICES

We can excerpt a few sample tasks from the list in Figure 1.5.3 in order to test this thesis that selected responsibilities in the project process are more suited to autonomous technology than others. Choosing a few examples that are primarily procedural by using our classifications above, I speculate on how AI systems might work in concert with their human architectural counterparts.

What this quick sketch problem suggests is that, at least in the near term, AI systems will be limited in scope, require enormous amounts of what is currently unavailable data, and likely augment, rather than eliminate, the central jobs of architects. This is a reassuring conclusion in the near term, but bears further consideration as AI systems evolve, in theory, from empiricist to cognitive capabilities.

STANDARD SCOPES OF SERVICE				
RIBA (UK)	**0** STRATEGIC DEFINITION	**1** PREPARATION + BRIEFING	**2** CONCEPT DESIGN	**3** SPATIAL COORDINATION
AIA (US)	**PD** PRELIMINARY DESIGN, PROGRAMMING		**SD** SCHEMATIC DESIGN	**DD** DESIGN DEVELOPMENT

SERVICE CATEGORIES				
DEFINITION				
DESIGN				
PRODUCTION				
PROCUREMENT				
CONSTRUCTION				
OPERATION				

TASK COMPONENTS				
PRACTICE MANAGEMENT				
OBTAINING WORK				
GETTING, ASSIGNING, MANAGING STAFFING				
MONITORING PRACTICE FINANCIAL HEALTH				
SETTING BUSINESS STRATEGY				
MANAGING PRACTICE OPERATIONS				
PRACTICE MANAGEMENT AND COORDINATION				
MANAGING PROJECT STAFFING RESOURCES				
ASSIGNING AND COORDINATING WORK				
MAINTAINING BUDGETS AND SCHEDULES				
COORDINATING CONSULTANTS AND OTHERS				
IDEATION DESIGN GENERATION				
ANALYSING AND UNDERSTANDING THE BRIEF				
GENERATING ALTERNATIVES				
EVALUATING AND SELECTING ALTERNATIVES				
DOCUMENTING DESIGN DECISIONS				
RESOLVING CONFLICTING REQUIREMENTS				
TECHNICAL PRODUCTION AND ANALYSIS				
DETERMINING CONFORMANCE TO THE BRIEF				
EVALUATING AND INTERGRATING TECHNICAL CONSIDERATIONS				
PERFORMING ENGINEERING ANALYSIS				
EVALUATING AND MANAGING PROJECT COSTS				
COORDINATING SPATIAL AND TECHNICAL SYSTEMS				
PRODUCING TECHNICAL DOCUMENTATION				
REVIEWING AND APPROVING TECHNICAL DOCUMENTS				
REVIEWING CONSTRUCTION PROGRESS				
CLIENT AND REGULATORY MANAGEMENT				
MEETING, MANAGING CLIENTS/DECISIONS				
COORDINATING WITH REGULATORS				
INTERFACING WITH PUBLIC/COMMUNITIES				

4 TECHNICAL DESIGN	NOT USED	5 MANUFACTURING + CONSTRUCTION	6 HANDOVER	7 USE
CD CONSTRUCTION DOCUMENTS	PR PROCUREMENT	CA CONSTRUCTION CONTRACT ADMIN	NOT USED	POE POST OCCUPANCY EVALUATION

1.5.3:
TASK COMPONENTS IN TRADITIONAL SCOPES OF SERVICE

Legend:

- PROCEDURAL
- PROCEDURAL TO INTEGRATIVE
- INTEGRATIVE
- INTEGRATIVE TO PERCEPTIVE
- PERCEPTIVE

TASK COMPONENT	GOAL	METRIC	PROPOSED AI
PRACTICE MANAGEMENT			
OBTAINING WORK	CAPTURE AS MANY NEW PROJECTS AS POSSIBLE	WIN RATE	MONITORS SUSPECT AND PROSPECT PROJECTS, DETERMINES KEY CHARACTERISTICS, TAGS PROJECTS THAT ARE MORE LIKELY TO BE OBTAINED.
GETTING, ASSIGNING, MANAGING STAFFING	OPTIMISE THE USE OF STAFF ACROSS ASSIGNMENTS	STAFF UTILISATION	EXAMINES STAFFING ASSIGNMENTS OF ALL PAST PROJECTS, PROPOSES STAFF BY TASKS, IDENTIFIES EMERGENT PROBLEMS.
MONITORING PRACTICE FINANCIAL HEALTH	ASSURE FINANCIAL HEALTH	PROFIT AND OVERHEAD	EVALUATES ALL PAST PROJECT MANAGEMENT RECORDS, SUPPORTS FEE PROPOSALS, FLAGS PROBLEMS IN OPERATION PROJECTS
PROJECT MANAGEMENT AND COORDINATION			
MAINTAINING BUDGETS AND SCHEDULES	CONFORM PROJECT TIME, STAFF AND FINANCIAL RESOURCES ARE ALIGNED	HOURLY RATE, TARGET PROFIT BY PROJECT, UTILISATION	BASED ON PAST PERFORMANCE, MONITORS PROJECT OPERATIONS, PROJECTS OVERRUNS AND CONFLICTS, PROJECTS PROFIT, RECOMMENDS CORRECTIONS
COORDINATING CONSULTANTS AND OTHERS	ASSURE CONSULTANTS PERFORM THEIR WORK ACCURATELY AND TIMELY	DELIVERABLE SCHEDULES	MONITORS TIMING AND DETAIL OF CONSULTANT SUBMISSIONS, RECOMMENDS TIMING OF SUBMISSIONS, FLAGS DISCONTINUITIES
IDEATION, DESIGN GENERATION			
GENERATING ALTERNATIVES	EXPLORE THE SOLUTION OPPORTUNITIES	NUMBER OF VIABLE ALTERNATIVES	RECOMMENDS VARIABLES BASED ON PROJECT TYPE, EVALUATES PREVIOUS SELECTED SCHEMES, EXCERPTS SUCCESSFUL SUB-COMPONENTS, DEFINES SOLUTION SPACE

TASK COMPONENT	GOAL	METRIC	PROPOSED AI
IDEATION, DESIGN GENERATION			
EVALUATING AND SELECTING ALTERNATIVES	FIND THE BEST ALTERNATIVE SOLUTIONS	NUMBER OF VIABLE ALTERNATIVES	HELPS EVALUATE TRADE-OFFS, DETERMINES PROMISING PATTERNS IN ALTERNATIVE GENERATION, PROVIDES OBJECTIVE EVALUATION OF SOLUTIONS
TECHNICAL PRODUCTION AND ANALYSIS			
DETERMINING CONFORMANCE TO THE BRIEF	CONFIRM THE DESIGN CONFORMS TO THE PERFORMANCE TARGETS IN THE BRIEF	VARIANCE FROM BRIEF PARAMETERS (AREA, BUDGET, VOLUME)	EXAMINES DESIGN DELIVERABLES AND MAPS TO PERFORMANCE PARAMETERS OF THE BRIEF AND FLAGS DISCONTINUITIES; RECOMMENDS REMEDIATION BASED ON PAST SOLUTIONS
EVALUATING AND MANAGING PROJECT COSTS	ASSURE THE PROJECT CONFORMS TO THE CONSTRUCTION BUDGET	TARGET VALUE OR CONSTRUCTION COST TARGET BUDGET	GENERATES ESTIMATES, MONITORS CONFORMANCE, RECOMMENDS COST ALIGNMENT STRATEGIES
COORDINATING SPATIAL AND TECHNICAL SYSTEMS	ASSURE SYSTEMS WORK IN 3D SPACE IN CONCERT	VALID CONFLICTS AND INTERFERENCES	IDENTIFIES SPATIAL CONFLICTS, SOLVES SIMPLE PROBLEMS, ELIMINATES INVALID CONFLICTS, SUGGESTS SOLUTIONS FOR IMPORTANT CONFLICTS
REVIEWING CONSTRUCTION PROGRESS	ALIGN CONSTRUCTION PROGRESS WITH TIME AND PAYMENT SCHEDULES	PERCENTAGE OF CONSTRUCTION COMPLETION, ACCURACY OF INSTALLATION	EVALUATES INPUTS FROM CONSTRUCTION SITE, IDENTIFIES INSTALLATION DISCONTINUITIES, COMPUTES VALUES OF INSTALLATION, ASSESSES CONSTRUCTION COMPLETE
CLIENT AND REGULATORY MANAGEMENT			
COORDINATING WITH REGULATORS	ASSURE THE PROJECT CONFORMS TO REGULATORY CONSTRAINTS	PERMITS AND APPROVALS ACHIEVED	EVALUATES CODE CONFORMANCE, IDENTIFIES DISCONTINUITIES, RECOMMENDS VARIANCES

PRESENT, NEAR FUTURE AND BEYOND

Empiricist AI systems that subscribe to the Susskind definition are beginning to appear in today's 'BuildTech' marketplace, and many focus on narrowly drawn procedures that demand clearly measurable goals, explicit logic and plenty of data. The table below describes a selection of some of these companies that are emerging as of mid-2021:

1.5.5:
AI-BASED
START-UPS IN
ARCHITECTURE,
2021

COMPANY	GOAL	LOGIC	DATA
SPACEMAKER AI	OPTIMISE MULTI-UNIT BUILDING CONFIGURATIONS ON A SITE	ADJUST BUILDING DIMENSIONAL PARAMETERS TO OPTIMISE USE AND CONFIGURATION	SITE PLANS AND ANALYTICAL OUTPUTS OF SPACE USE
PLANIT IMPACT	MEASURE AND REDUCE ENERGY AND WATER USE IN A BUILDING	TRANSLATE BUILDING CHARACTERISTICS INTO ENERGY AND STORMWATER INPUTS AND OUTPUTS	ENERGY MODELS, USAGE DATA, SITE INFRASTRUCTURE INFORMATION
JOIN	ORGANISE, OPTIMISE, AND CONTROL PROJECT CONSTRUCTION COSTS FROM CONCEPT TO COMPLETION	ANALYSE AND MANAGE COST INPUTS AND PROJECT HISTORY TOWARD COST TARGETS	COST ESTIMATING HISTORY, LOCAL ECONOMIC CONDITIONS, MARKET INFORMATION
ENVELOPE	DETERMINE THE MAXIMUM ALLOWABLE BUILDABLE AREA ON AN URBAN SITE	TRANSLATE BUILDING ZONING REGULATIONS IN TO BUILDING CONFIGURATIONS	ZONING CODES, PARAMETRIC BUILDING TEMPLATES

As these systems become more capable, collecting data and building complex, correlative data structures within their neural networks, it is likely that their logics will expand to a wider range of targeted tasks across the architect's responsibilities. Russell suggests that new ideas were often attributable to 'the three ineffable I's: intuition, insight, and inspiration'.[11] Procedural AI will augment these critical (perceptual) components of professional judgement, making the architect's services increasingly reliant upon, and validated by, analysis and data. One can imagine a day where the architect, having fully explored a range of options for the configuration of site – including the resulting performance data about rental area, storm water draining, zoning conformance and even construction cost – can recommend with greater confidence a decision that they chose with the assistance of a procedural AI. These systems will remain, however, limited to the lower rungs of Bloom's ladder of higher order thinking – analysis, with perhaps a touch of evaluation – since creation will continue to require the integration of a wide range of information, decisions and competency. Empirical AI is highly unlikely to reach the top rung.

Beyond the near-term future, the architect's services will need to respond to an evolving set of new expectations and constraints, including:

» the automation of construction

» the increased use of data across all enterprises including those of clients, and

» higher order design aspirations of social equity, environmental justice and epidemiological safety.

Few of the required services that architects will need to provide to address these needs can be found in the traditional methodologies of today, be it through the RIBA Plan of Work or the AIA's definition of 'Basic Services'. Deeper analytical insight, deployment of broad data evaluation and coordination of the data-driven tasks of a design team with varied (and ever-increasing) numbers of consultants will require architects to integrate the AIs that will support this work, in the same way in which they manage their engineers today. The challenges of design tomorrow will be best faced and conquered by people, masters of the ineffable I's, whose ideas will drive the spaces, buildings and cities of tomorrow, even if we reach the distant goal of Domingos' Master Algorithm.

1.5.6:
SPACEMAKER
AI, RECENTLY
ACQUIRED BY
AUTODESK FOR
$240 MILLION

1.6 DELIVERY, MEANS AND METHODS

>> ARCHITECTS OPERATE IN THE SYSTEMS
OF PROJECT DELIVERY WITH SPECIFIC
RELATIONSHIPS AND OBLIGATIONS TO THEIR
CLIENTS, THEIR CONSULTING COLLABORATORS,
BUILDERS AND, ULTIMATELY, THE PUBLIC.
THEY DEPLOY A VARIETY OF TECHNICAL
SKILLS AND TOOLS, IN COMBINATION WITH
HEURISTIC STRATEGIES THAT COMBINE SKILLS
OF JUDGEMENT, INTUITION AND LEADERSHIP,
TO FULFIL THEIR RESPONSIBILITIES. HOW
DOES THE ROLE OF THE ARCHITECT AS A
PROFESSIONAL CHANGE AS TECHNOLOGY MOVES
TOWARD AUTONOMOUS COMPUTING? <<

SYSTEMS OF DELIVERY

The term 'project delivery' comprises two central aspects of making buildings:

1. The constellation of clients (who create demand for buildings and then operate and use them), architects (who design them) and constructors (who procure, fabricate, assemble and build them).
2. How those players are arrayed in a set of professional, informational, financial and legal relationships defined by their respective roles, responsibilities and ability to manage risk.

These two factors combine in typical ways according to a formal template known as a **project delivery model**.[1] In a perfect world, an appropriate delivery model would be determined that matched the demands of the project and the capabilities of the participants. However, since power dynamics and politics play as much a role in such decisions as technical considerations, the choice of a delivery system is not always perfectly suited to the players or the project itself, introducing informational discontinuities at the beginning of a project that often last for the duration, to little good effect.

PROJECT DELIVERY TYPOLOGIES

DESIGN BID BUILD	CONSTRUCTION MANAGEMENT	DESIGN BUILD/ NOVATION	INTEGRATED PROJECT DELIVERY
		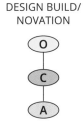	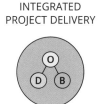

1.6.1: A SELECTION OF TYPICAL DELIVERY MODELS SEEN TODAY

Over the course of the 20th century, and particularly as architecture evolved into a bona fide profession, the key players in these delivery models developed prototypical roles. Clients look to convert capital into a physical asset, but lack the technical capability to do so, so they hire architects to define their needs and contractors to translate that definition into a building. For a variety of reasons that includes the misalignment of interests, these systems yield unsatisfactory results[2] and as such there has been extensive experimentation in reforming them.

As described in Chapter 1.3, that misalignment, combined with the prototypical roles of the architect and builder, sets each in opposition to the other. Architects deliver professional services in the form of judgement and are therefore largely in the business of creating and dispensing ideas (the design), whereas contractors deliver products, and as such are primarily tasked with making things (the building). These distinctions, in this context, are important. If architects have the role of 'proposing ideas' and contractors somehow 'disposing them', tensions will surely result. However, as the built environment becomes increasingly digitised, the divide between designer and builder feels unnecessarily artificial – serving neither the architect, builder, nor their mutual client. While the production of many of the products that drive the economy – automobiles, airplanes, consumer appliances, electronics – has been digitally optimised for decades, the construction industry has trailed far behind. This gap is beginning to close with the industrialisation of construction.[3]

Thus, the autonomous opportunities of artificial intelligence are likely to have an impact on both the services provided by architects in delivery systems and how those services are converted into physical artefacts of the built world.

The challenges of delivery dynamics in modern construction have been addressed by a variety of strategies, ranging from the reconfiguration of relationships between design, cost estimating, construction and suppliers as seen in models like public-private partnerships (PPP) and recent experimentation with integrated project delivery (IPD), to attempts at revolutionary means of joint design/construction representation like BIM – or even a combination of these together. The heart of the problem, however, was identified as early as 1963 in a report prepared for the UK construction industry:

> >> The basic decisions of construction control are often incomplete or unduly rushed because necessary information is not available sufficiently ahead of time, or is not complete enough. On many occasions members of the construction team could, but do not, ease this problem by supplying the data that would facilitate the preparation of fuller and more useful information by others. Building construction is remarkable among industrial activities for the lack of detailed information about how it proceeds. Until more is known there can be no basis for improvement.[4] <<

Each of the players working to deliver a project requires information at a specific level of resolution, at a certain time, and with a precise degree of completeness. Each creates, consumes, deploys and/or distributes this information in order to fulfil their obligations, make a profit and not assume unmanageable risk. Projects are thus delivered in a constellation of interdependent yet incompatible collections of information structures and responsibilities. In the digital age, various technologies lurk below the surface of delivery, hoping to smooth and improve it. AI is just now arriving to join that crowded field of suitors. We can expect AI to augment – yet also possibly replace – the capabilities of the architect, and to generate and organise the informational structures that connect architecture to construction.

DESIGN INTENT

At the centre of these questions is the definition of the architect's fundamental responsibility to the delivery process itself. That duty is best understood through a concept of 'design intent', defined by the RIBA Plan of Work as '(t)he means by which the design team describes a Building System in a manner that allows a specialist subcontractor to design the system'.[5] If you are wondering who, exactly, is the designer of any given system in a building, you are not alone. Architects and their collaborating consultants (engineers and the like) set out, at a level of detail necessary to be clear about their intentions (whatever that may mean), information about how the design should look and operate once it has been completed. There are numerous intermediate steps necessary before 'the design' is ready to be realised in the field, including the specifics of materials and assemblies, the exact procedures and processes of building (called the 'means and methods' of construction) and numerous other decisions made by the contractors, both big and small. Broadly generalising about the nature of modern construction on both sides of the Atlantic, it can be charitably concluded that construction has become too technically complex for a single entity – designers or builders – to be wholly responsible for it. Even the smallest project has a coterie of subcontractors, product manufacturers and material suppliers, and cost is always top of mind. In the most optimistic characterisation of the ideal arrangement under these rules of engagement, the architect sets out her ideas in sufficient detail to guide the builder, and the contractor figures out all the specific particulars. Much is lost in translation.

It was not always such. In the late 18th century in the UK, and as long as 100 years later in the US, the architect was wholly responsible for all aspects of construction. Higgin and Jessop described the project delivery model in Figure 1.6.2.

1.6.2:
PROJECT
DELIVERY IN
THE UK, 18TH
CENTURY[6]

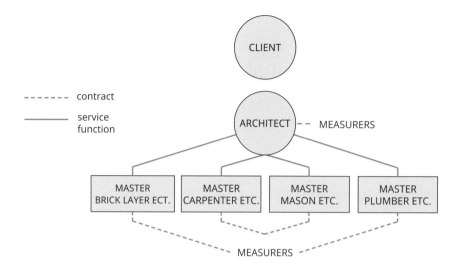

Alas, worries about and failures of project coordination and management of budgets, along with the increasing complexity of urban- and industrial-age construction, brought things more into current alignment by the 19th century[7], with only slight elaboration in the 20th, as seen in Figure 1.6.3.

Note the appearance of the quantity surveyor (to manage costs) and the main contractor (to procure and coordinate the work), both roles that reflect current practice. As these models evolved, the level of granularity and resolution of information necessary to build ever increased, and it became apparent that as the project's interface with the procurement process, the contractor and her minions – including subcontractors who would fabricate building systems – was best to 'finalise' the design itself.[8]

As the building industry has moved from drawings to BIM, the inherent tensions of such a system were exacerbated rather than calmed by the availability of 3D information. Architects complained that they had neither the expertise nor the fee to provide extreme construction detail in their design intent BIM data, and builders declared that the resulting BIM deliverables were unsuitable for building. So despite the insertion of a technology designed to increase transparency and collaboration, the age-old pathologies persist.

Yet there are other forces at play that may, through technology, finally close this ancient divide. In a market that is increasingly pressed towards more

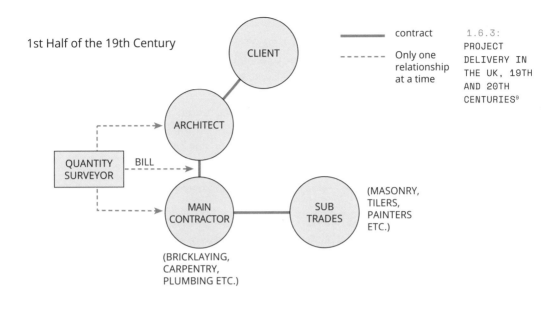

1st Half of the 19th Century

———— contract

- - - - - Only one relationship at a time

1.6.3:
PROJECT DELIVERY IN THE UK, 19TH AND 20TH CENTURIES[9]

(MASONRY, TILERS, PAINTERS ETC.)

(BRICKLAYING, CARPENTRY, PLUMBING ETC.)

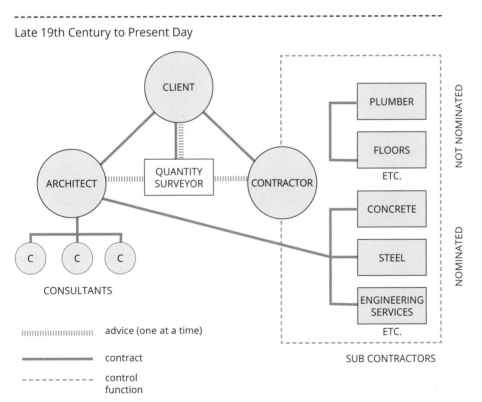

Late 19th Century to Present Day

|||||||||||||||||| advice (one at a time)

———— contract

- - - - - control function

SUB CONTRACTORS

efficiency and productivity, and dissatisfied with the results of traditional delivery approaches, the move to digital fabrication and industrial processes in construction is inevitable. This is particularly true as automation moves the industry towards what is now being called 'industrialised construction' and accelerated using manufacturing strategies for building.[10] There is an obvious, resulting demand for higher quality digital deliverables to smooth the path. However, will architects and their consulting engineers deliver them? And can AI play a part in closing the professional divide?

PROFESSIONAL RELATIONSHIPS

This question must be examined in the context of all the obligations of the architect, informational and otherwise. To do so, we can turn the traditional delivery model diagrams found in Figure 1.6.1 inside-out to look at the specific connections of the architect in any such structure, depicted in Figure 1.6.2. With our hypothetical architect in the middle of her relationships, we can see four distinct roles required (see Figure 1.6.4).

An agent of the owner, who acts as the client's intermediary in the process, generating the design and stewarding it, armed with descriptions of her 'design intent', through construction and acting as the owner's proxy to assure the building conforms to that intent.

A leader of the design team, who orchestrates and integrates the work of various consultancies in the service of creating a coherent, coordinated and accurate design which will be passed along to the builders.

A guide to the builder, to articulate the goals of the project and help the construction team to interpret, clarify and ultimately review and approve the design intent on behalf of the client as it is translated into more detailed information to support construction. A subcontractor, responsible for a given building system, will often create very detailed information in support of the fabrication of that system (shop drawings) but the architect must review and approve such proposals before the fabricator may begin.

A protector of the public, including both the specific users of the project as well as those with whom the architect has no specific contractual obligations but nonetheless is responsible for the health, safety and welfare of those who inhabit her design.

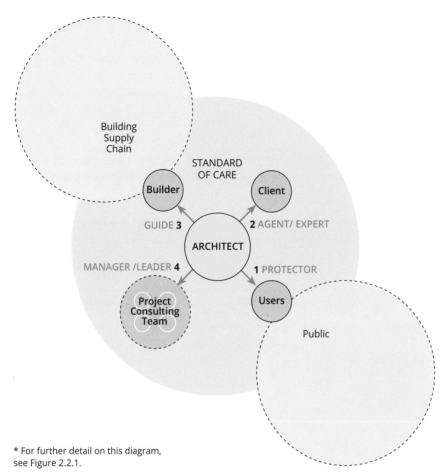

* For further detail on this diagram,
see Figure 2.2.1.

The architect thus either generates, reviews or is subject to the implications of the vast amounts of information that swirl around even a simple building enterprise. That information, despite efforts to rigorously standardise it, manifests in a wide variety of formats, versions and levels of detail, and must be understood, coordinated and often translated from source to recipient to be useful. An immediate opportunity of AI – one that is yet unexplored as of this writing – would be to try to 'understand' the relationships between these data and help deploy them in a structured, accessible and efficient manner.

RELATIONSHIPS, DELIVERY AND COMPUTATION

So perhaps AI will one day rationalise the ebbs and flows of digital information that follow the relationships and obligations of the architect as a project is delivered. If enough data can be organised and made accessible, this would seem a prime opportunity for the next generation of empiricist, deep-learning systems that are so good at finding patterns and connections between data points.

But how might AI, in the immediate future, either augment or eliminate the jobs of architects as defined in these four roles? Some early speculation is summarised in Table 1.6.5.

1.6.5:
EXAMPLE
OF AI
IMPLICATIONS
FOR THE
DELIVERY
ROLE OF THE
ARCHITECT

ROLE	AUGMENTATION BY AI	ELIMINATION BY AI
AGENT OF THE OWNER	DEMONSTRATED DESIGN RESULTS BASED ON LARGE REPRESENTATIVE DATA AND AI-GENERATED CONCLUSIONS	GENERATION OF COMPLETE DESIGN SCHEMES
LEADER OF THE DESIGN TEAM	COHERENT DISTRIBUTION OF USEFUL INFORMATION TO THE POINT OF WORK	INTEGRATION OF ENGINEERING AND OTHER REPRESENTATIONS OF THE PROJECT AND COORDINATION OF THEIR WORK
GUIDE TO THE DESIGN INFORMATION TO THE BUILDER	DESIGN DATA AUGMENTED BY PROCEDURAL INFORMATION FOR ASSEMBLY AND CONSTRUCTION	AUTOMATIC GENERATION OF CONSTRUCTION DOCUMENTATION, BASED ON INFORMATION DEMANDS OF THE BUILDER
PROTECTOR OF THE PUBLIC'S HEALTH, SAFETY AND WELFARE	LIFE SAFETY ANALYSIS AND COMPLIANCE EVALUATION	CODE CHECKING AND CERTIFICATION FOR PERMIT

The importance of guiding the development and outcomes of emergent AI systems is apparent in the contrasts between augmentation and elimination scenarios. While autonomous algorithms may help architects to generate alternatives and evaluate them, it is technically a very short step to allowing those systems to make final decisions about the design, essentially leaving the architect (or someone else) as just the operator. Less likely is the possibility that the coordination of the design team itself would be entirely replaced by automation, as this task is as much about human leadership as technical integration. The move towards industrialised construction creates demand for far more data than just traditional 'design intent', in the form of higher resolution design data and procedural templates for sequences of fabrication and assembly. These may be automated by virtue of intelligent algorithms in the future and have the potential to eliminate huge swathes of the architect's role – and compensation – as a result. Finally, in what is perhaps a central existential threat that will be examined in Chapter 2.3, the architect's fundamental responsibility for the public's health, safety and welfare, as defined by the understanding, interpretation and implementation of planning and safety codes, is being automated by companies like UpCodes even today. Once that job is done by computers, the need for professional certification by a person – rather than a machine – is called into question.

MEANS AND METHODS

So it appears now that design, construction, and building operation processes are rapidly digitising; that the obligations of the players in delivery are likely to evolve accordingly, particularly those of designers and builders; that these processes are creating a lot of data that could be consumed by hungry AI systems looking to learn how to (charitably) help; and that the biggest gulf in the digital divide is between design and construction, especially as construction becomes more like manufacturing.

So what is the most useful focus for AI in delivery from the architect's perspective? Automation algorithms are good at memorialising processes (like how to count the number of windows in a building), empiricist autonomous processes are good at examining data for patterns and, eventually, cognitive systems might stitch the two together. Bridging the gap from design intent to construction execution is the most likely target of the combination of all of these AI-based technological options, in that it will require a broad set of capabilities beyond a single technology and could, potentially, improve the overall delivery of projects in the most dramatic and immediate way.

As BIM was beginning to focus the attention of the building industry on process revolution, the labour theorist, Paolo Tombesi, put forth a proposition about the changing role of the architect called 'flexible specialisation'. He argued that the making of a building – in essence, the underlying delivery model – was comprised of a constellation of processes and obligations which required the technical and synthetic design skills of an architect, and as such the profession should move away from slavish dedication to the design of objects to a broader, more dynamic set of responsibilities in project delivery (see Figure 1.6.6).[11]

While Tombesi did not speculate beyond the technological possibilities of BIM, his argument extends easily to circumstances where certain data and procedural aspects of his process nodes are automated in part by AI, and the architect assumes the role of deploying these capabilities to orchestrate and integrate the results. Further, the variety of data flows implied by delivery structure of flexible specialisation demand a rationalising platform to organise, normalise and monitor that information, a powerful potential use of AI's capabilities.

Finally, beyond the immediate interdependent processes of construction lies an extensive supply chain of both raw and processed materials. The architect and historian, Andrew Rabeneck, has gone so far as to argue that designers and builders are mere 'contingent players with the new political economy' of the capital flows of construction commodities such as steel or cement.[12] Control of the intellectual property of industrial production was, according to Rabeneck, assumed by those who took on the risk of development of those systems and, as a result, 'industrial control over scientific knowledge and processes grew steadily among material and product manufacturing companies'.[13] He extends this argument to suggest that this shifting of knowledge and understanding of the supply chain and its components is part of the larger loss of value and influence of architects themselves.

As the means and methods of construction are increasingly industrialised, it is possible that Rabeneck's purported professional descent of architectural prowess may accelerate, further widening the gap between intent and execution. This possibility strengthens the argument that the tools of AI – which could significantly enhance the architect's understanding of the processes, procedures and informational requirements of construction, and allow that insight to inform and support design – can be deployed to either augment or eliminate the architect in the systems of delivery.

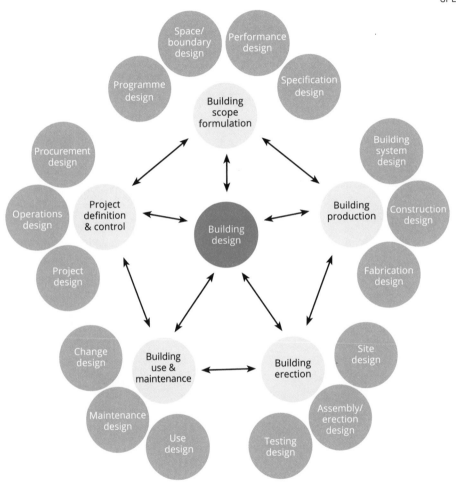

02
RELATION-SHIPS

>> THE BUILDING ENTERPRISE DEPENDS UPON A SERIES OF NETWORKS ACTUALISED TO YIELD RESULTS. PROFESSIONAL TEAMS OF CONSULTANTS AND BUILDERS ARE ONE SUCH NETWORK; THEIR RISK RELATIONSHIPS, ECONOMIC EXCHANGES AND DATA NETWORKS ARE OTHER EXAMPLES. HOWEVER, A THIRD SET OF NETWORKS – THE NEURAL NETWORKS THAT COMPRISE AI/ML SYSTEMS – WILL SOON OVERLAY THESE STRUCTURES AND TRANSFORM THEM. <<

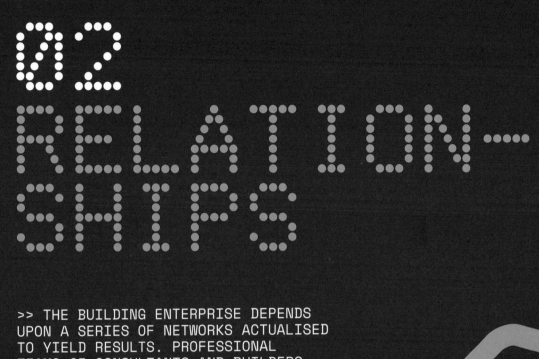

2.1 ECONOMICS, COMPENSATION AND VALUE

>> LIKE ALL TECHNOLOGY, AI IS LIKELY
TO PROVIDE NEW OPPORTUNITIES FOR
VALUE CREATION AND PRODUCTIVITY WHILE
SIMULTANEOUSLY ELIMINATING THE NEED
FOR SOME TASKS PERFORMED BY HUMAN
ARCHITECTS. THE DANGERS OF TRADITIONAL
PRESSURES OF COMMODIFICATION MIGHT BE
OFFSET BY NEW CAPABILITIES, AND WITH
THOSE CAPABILITIES, NEW OPPORTUNITIES
TO DELIVER VALUE — AND INCREASE
PROFITABILITY — IN PRACTICE. <<

Architects operate within the larger economic models of the building industry, which has long struggled to create consistent value propositions for its participants. Most buildings are produced under an economic dictum: achieve the end product by optimising for the single variable of lowest first cost. Clients often select architects by arbitraging fees for the lowest price; architects then choose their consulting engineers in the same way. Contractors are often chosen based upon lowest bid, passing that logic down the entire supply chain to the far reaches of building product manufacturers, fabricators and suppliers. The value of the resulting project to the participants in its creation or, ultimately, the client, is not reflected in the economic deals that actualise it. As artificial intelligence changes the capabilities, obligations and outcomes of project architects, how might the economic propositions evolve accordingly?

CANONICAL MODELS

As came to be understood during the first Industrial Revolution, technology disrupts patterns of employment and pay. Mechanised farm equipment displaced plough drivers and their oxen, and industrialised looms put hand weavers out of business. This is a version of 'creative destruction', as defined by the Austrian economist Joseph Schumpeter in the mid-20th century, where new economic systems – often catalysed by new technologies – destroy and replace their predecessors, presumably improving economic performance for everyone while doing so.[1] And although these improvements may prove temporary, as new competitors touting newer technologies enter the fray, the concept of creative destruction advancing the marketplace can be paired with the so-called 'canonical model' of employment described by Daniel Susskind, where 'it was *impossible* for new technologies to make either skilled or unskilled workers worse off; technological progress always raised everyone's wages, though at a given time some more than others'.[2]

If artificial intelligence is the catalyst for creative destruction in the practice of architecture, then one can conclude that design jobs will be eliminated by the capabilities it presumably assumes. The canonical economic model argues, however, that those jobs are more than replaced by new ones necessary to support the creation and support of the new technologies. So you might have lost your job working in an architect's office doing zoning and code analysis and planning studies, but you (or someone else) will surely be hired by one of the many AI-based companies creating software to do that particular task.[3] And, in theory at least, the quality of the resulting design work created by the surviving practitioners will improve by virtue of the tremendous new capabilities of software-assisted design, and the cost of your house or school will decline as a result.

Those challenges are heightened by the possibilities of AI-related replacement. Susskind further argues in *A World Without Work* that it is not entire jobs that will be supplanted by AI, but rather specific tasks within those jobs. He suggests that technology will continue to spread the gap between skilled labour (not easily replaced by machines) and unskilled jobs (where many tasks may be automated). Architects are generally considered skilled workers, but there are broad swathes of our jobs subject to such automation, as suggested in Figure 1.5.3.

The challenge, as always, is converting that resulting potency into actual value that is reflected in the economics of practice. Technology notwithstanding, it has always been difficult for architects to both improve the quality of our services and the amount of money we are paid to provide them.

EFFICIENCY AND EFFECTIVENESS

Two relatively recent technological shifts in practice demonstrate this difficulty. As computer-aided drafting tools such as AutoCAD© came to the fore, largely in the early 1990s, the capital investment in both hardware and software was significant.[4] To defray these costs, firms often would charge clients an hourly fee for 'CAD services' that was treated as a project expense not unlike travel or blueprinting. Over time, however, clients got wise to this idea and refused to pay these charges, arguing that the benefits of the computer's precision and efficiency accrued to the architect, not themselves. Of course, this point of view did not reflect the greater accuracy or consistency of CAD-generated deliverables, nor the increased complexity of design solutions they were able to create, and architects (once again) failed to convert the improvement in the quality of their services to an increase in their fees, which continued to be pressured by lowest-first-cost competition.

The second technological wave brought along by BIM had similar, if structurally distinct, results, at least here in the United States. Figure 2.1.2 documents performance of the American architectural profession in the two years on either side of the great economic crisis of 2009. Net revenue for all AIA firms in 2005 was approximately $27 billion, and the profession had returned to 96% of that revenue number ($26.4 billion) by 2013, signalling a

2.1.1:
A HAPPY CAD
OPERATOR AT
HIS STATION
IN THE
OFFICES OF
CESAR PELLI
& ASSOCIATES
(NOW PELLI
CLARKE PELLI
ARCHITECTS),
C. 2000

recovery. If net revenue is a rough proxy for work produced, then that same amount of effort was produced by 16,000 fewer employees (about 11%) at the same time that BIM adoption rose almost four-fold:

YEAR	NET REVENUE ($ BILLIONS)	PERCENTAGE OF FIRMS USING BIM ON BILLABLE PROJECTS	NUMBER OF ARCHITECTURAL POSITIONS
2005	27.5	10%	115,9000
2013	26.4	37%	99,800

2.1.2:
COMPARING
REVENUE, BIM
ADOPTION AND
EMPLOYMENT IN
TWO RECENT
YEARS[5]

What the data seems to suggest is that these architects increased their productive capacity, presumably by use of newer technology, by over 10% by producing the same amount of work with far fewer people. Anecdotal data from practitioners indicate that while work volume increased steadily after the Crisis, fee multiples stayed depressed, suggesting that these numbers may not completely reflect the productivity gains of BIM technology. A more careful analysis mapping profits, BIM adoption and a proxy for productivity (net fee revenue per employee) in Figure 2.1.3 indicates that productivity accelerates with BIM adoption but, sadly, profitability is unrelated. A missed opportunity to be sure.

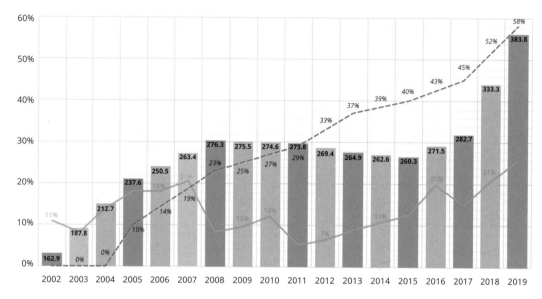

Comparison of Production, Profit and BIM Adoption in the US–2002 through 2019

■ Net Fee Revenue per Billable Employee ($000)　── Firm Profitablity　── ── Percentage of BIM Adoption

2.1.3:
PRODUCTIVITY,
PROFITABILITY
AND BIM
ADOPTION[6]

So, here is a case where new technology (BIM) brought new capabilities and efficiencies, yet it appears the profession did not directly benefit in any tangible, economic way. If AI has similar implications, essentially shrinking the commoditised value of the architect's services, a radically enfeebled profession is likely to result. However, there are at least three strategies – automation, analysis and prediction – made possible by the technical potency of emergent AI that could help us to avoid this fate.

PRODUCTIVITY REDEFINED

The analysis above is an invented proxy for the putative improvements in architectural productivity in the correlation between technology adoption (the instrumentation) and the number of staff positions necessary to generate a certain fee volume. There are no generally accepted measures for determining such productivity, a result of both the intractable nature of the design process and a general lack of attention of researchers to such questions, particularly those in the professional associations.[7] In my professional practice courses, I pose this question slightly differently: if you are a manager of a design process, exactly how long does it take to have a good idea, and then produce it? If design is a process of solving Horst Rittel's 'wicked problems', then the 'wicked' nature of the process itself makes it difficult to precisely answer this question, making the resulting projections of time, effort and expense similarly intractable.

So perhaps any intelligent strategy for deploying AI tools for increased productivity should take a different tack, in three dimensions – automation, analysis and prediction – by combining the capabilities of AI as defined by Greaves in Chapter 1.2, Figure 1.2.4.

> **Automation** is intelligently replacing linear processes currently performed by humans with AI-assisted algorithms that might learn those capabilities as they 'see' more examples.

> **Analysis** is creating more sophisticated means to measure and understand the results and implications of a design decision.

> **Prediction** is combining the capabilities of automation and analysis to project a final result of such a decision, and in doing so learning, by virtue of selections made by human designers, how to both select and optimise a result.

The diagram in Figure 2.1.4 sketches this relationship by examining a process realm ripe for technology-driven productivity: checking a building design for code compliance.

The hypothetical designer of this AI-enabled future is struggling to validate the building code compliance of her design, and is deploying a progressively capable set of machine learning algorithms, which we will call a 'Code Evaluation System', that combine both cognitive and empiricist strategies. Early in the life of this system she has created a design, probably in BIM, so the components can be easily identified spatially and typologically. The system first identifies all the relevant life safety components relative to, say, fire exiting, in her model; in this case, the doors and stairs, all of which must be properly sized, oriented and configured. If the AI missed a component, the architect identifies it manually, and the AI identifier learns over time to better find and understand those elements.

Once this system has learned to find all the pieces of the building's existing components, it can move to 'Part 2' of this process – applying evaluative algorithms to analyse the actual behaviour of each of the elements of the

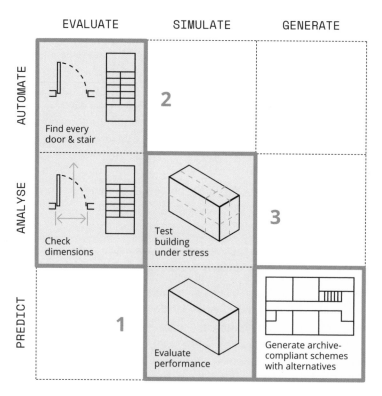

design. Do the doors swing in the right direction? Do they have the proper fire ratings? Are the stairs properly configured, within protective enclosures, large enough to handle the number of occupants? This is the intersection of automation, analysis and evaluation in Greaves's terms, indicated in the diagrams as 'Part 1'.

Our machine learning Code Evaluation System is starting, with a combination of rules-based algorithms and practice with its human operator, to learn about the interaction of architectural elements necessary to make a safe building. By extending this system with additional simulative capabilities – an overlay of fire spread, smoke distribution and occupancy behaviour – it can move from the evaluation of individual elements to the behaviour of an entire building, evaluating the comprehensive performance of that building under the simulated conditions of duress. This is the intersection of analysis and prediction with simulations, in Greaves's terms, or 'Part 2' of the evolution of our system.

In the ultimate manifestation of this proposed system, 'Part 3' in our diagram, the system has assembled a sufficiently robust understanding of the combined characteristics of safe conditions in a building so that it has limited, but ever-expanding, capabilities to generate a series of safety solutions from the preliminary model presented by its architect master. If a number of such architects are training such a progressively capable system, it will 'learn' over time to optimise the answers.

The system proposed here has several salient characteristics:

»   It is working on a discrete problem that is vexing, technical and measurable in result.

»   It is solving problems that do not implicate the architect's design abilities.

»   If it works well, it saves time, effort and brainpower for the architect, who can then, in theory, either convert the resulting work cycles into profit (by simply cashing them) or by applying them to improve the 'wicked' characteristics of the design itself. Either way, this architect has converted the capabilities of her new AI-enabled design assistant into value, economic or otherwise.[8]

BEYOND PRODUCTIVITY AND PERFORMANCE

A sufficiently effective set of AI tools, capable of both optioneering and accurate prediction, brings the architect's value proposition into an entirely new realm, entirely decoupling compensation from the value of time sold and allowing designers to be paid on the basis of the resulting performance of their buildings. This is a tricky but potentially lucrative strategy where design services are no longer a commoditised transaction in the delivery chain, but rather tied closely to project behaviour. The resulting promises should not be bound to issues of beauty, experience or aesthetics, but rather to the sorts of technical behaviour that computers could be trained, over time, to accurately predict.

Productivity and process strategies notwithstanding, another immediate value opportunity in a world increasingly dependent upon AI is the fuel for that process itself – data, sometimes called 'the new oil'.[9] The building industry is notorious for a lack of data standards, repositories or means for shared access across its participants. Yet there is a hierarchy of provocative data that will accumulate across the various dimensions of the building enterprise itself, described graphically in Figure 2.1.5.

For our purposes, the centre of this universe is the data collected within the architect's office itself, which in sufficient quantity might be useful to the firm in improving the capabilities of its AI systems. However, since such systems require enormous amounts of data, it is more likely that architectural data per se would be collected among the profession itself. Beyond that, training and reference data for machine learning platforms could be aggregated at project level, say by building type, or even across the design-to-build marketplace. Eventually, all such data could exist in the context of the overall building industry, including design, construction, procurement and operational information, ultimately referenceable across all the players implementing AI.

2.1.5:
DATA
REALMS
WITH
EXCHANGE
VALUE IN
AECO

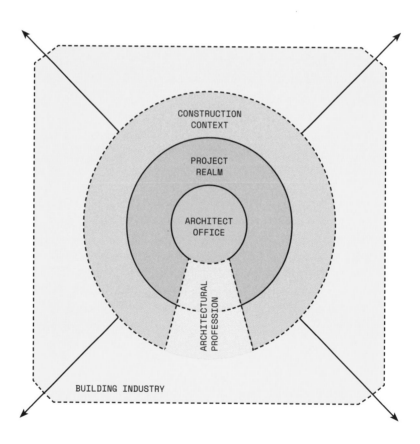

There is a tremendous economic value in such a proposed data reserve, both as a source of insight and as employment. Training AI systems requires coherent, consistent, 'clean' data and it has been argued that conforming data requires as much, if not more, effort than building the AI software itself.[10] As the 'canonical model' suggests, curating and managing this data is a likely source of employment for architects, new roles emerging from the resulting creative destruction.

Such data should not, however, be simply gifted to the industry, as it has tremendous inherent value as well as potential risk of misuse. The creation of a data trust, mediated and managed by an independent, non-profit third party, could create the necessary platform for what will likely be huge amounts of digital building information that will be created in the future, fodder for capable AI systems.[11]

ALTERNATIVE ECONOMIC MODELS

If Susskind is right, the next decade will see an array of architectural tasks augmented, and in many cases supplanted, by AI systems. Whether entire jobs will be replaced as a result is the subject of some debate. Mastering a game like chess or Go – with very specific rules, precedents and a highly constrained context – is hardly a precondition for managing the various tasks, responsibilities and synthetic processes that comprise the abilities of any capable architect. It may be that, in the aggregate, the production and analytic functions of practice will be replaced by autonomous computation to an extent that fewer architects will be required to design the world's environment. However, conversely, perhaps, released from the drudgery of the mundane, the power of designers will intensify sufficiently so that the influence and importance of architects and architecture will expand by virtue of technology rather than be diminished by it. Careful and purposeful planning at the intersection of technological innovation and process improvement is the only way to make such an outcome a reality.

2.2 LAWS, POLICY AND RISK

>> ARCHITECTS HAVE TRADITIONALLY
BEEN HELD TO A COMMON LAW STANDARD
OF REASONABLE CARE, BASED ON THEIR
RESPONSIBILITY TO EXERCISE GOOD
JUDGEMENT IN CONTEXT. AS THOSE
RESPONSIBILITIES EVOLVE WITH MORE
INTELLIGENT TECHNOLOGY, HOW MIGHT LEGAL
STANDARDS, PUBLIC POLICY WITH REGARD
TO BUILDING AND THE PERFORMANCE OF THE
ARCHITECT CHANGE ACCORDINGLY? <<

While we await a wave of intelligent machines to change the architectural profession, AI/ML technology is already in wide use to set insurance rates, evaluate radiographic images, determine eligibility for loans and other government benefits, even capture suspected criminals with facial recognition. And given the inscrutable nature of these algorithms, which 'teach themselves' to generate results from pools of data (like hundreds of thousands of insurance claims, or even millions of portraits of potential criminals scraped from the internet), it is impossible to unpack the underlying logic by which they make decisions. Worse, that logic is barely comprehensible to the professionals that deploy it.

Attorney Michele Gilman represents indigent patients fighting for their rights in the opaque US health system, a bureaucracy made even more impenetrable now by its use of AI to allocate resources. This was exhibited in a recent case in Baltimore, Maryland, as described in a recent article in *MIT Technology Review*:

>> *Not until they were standing in the courtroom in the middle of a hearing did the witness representing the state reveal that the government had just adopted a new algorithm. The witness, a nurse, couldn't explain anything about it. 'Of course not – they bought it off the shelf,' Gilman says. 'At least she's a nurse, not a computer scientist. She couldn't answer what factors go into it. How is it weighted? What are the outcomes that you're looking for? So there I am with my student attorney, who's in my clinic with me, and it's like, "Oh, am I going to cross-examine an algorithm?"'* [1] <<

This vignette elegantly captures the range of challenges that the regulators, the public, the courts, architects and their clients face as the work of professionals is automated: who or what is responsible for the implications of decisions made by machines, and can they ever be sufficiently understood to place the public's welfare in their care?

THE DUTY OF CARE AND ITS RISKS

The United Kingdom and United States share a common law tradition establishing the competency standard for architects (emphasis added):

>> *The Architect/Consultant will exercise* **the reasonable skill, care and diligence** *to be expected of an Architect/Consultant experienced in the provision of such services for projects of a similar size, nature and complexity to the Project. (RIBA Standard Professional Services Contract 2018: Architectural Services)[2]*

The Architect shall perform its services consistent with the **professional skill and care ordinarily provided** *by architects practicing in the same or similar locality under the same or similar circumstances. The Architect shall perform its services as expeditiously as is consistent with such professional skill and care and the orderly progress of the Project. (AIA Document B101–2017: Standard Form of Agreement Between Owner and Architect)[3]* <<

In each case, the measure of the architect's performance is how it might compare to that of other competent practitioners in the same circumstances. This standard is not delineated by statute in any other form, but rather determined in a court of law after testimony by expert witnesses who posit correct professional behaviour and application of appropriate precedent.

As examined in Chapter 1.3, the relationship between architects and the public is essentially an exchange of trust: architects are empowered to make important decisions about the public's health, safety and welfare, and as such enjoy special privileges of this professional status; presumably influence, autonomy and compensation. In exchange, they must take personal responsibility for their actions and cannot delegate that responsibility in the manner of corporations, where the company, rather than the individual, is culpable for bad decisions.

Public policy dictates that a design professional be involved in a building project precisely to assure that the public's welfare is protected in the built environment and, at least for now, there is a responsible person held accountable. The requirements differ slightly between the US and the UK: in the latter, a 'principal designer' must be specified for any project involving more than one construction contractor[4] whereas in most US jurisdictions, a licensed architect must design any building for human habitation larger than approximately 275 sqm.[5]

In performing her duties, the architect assumes two types of risk:

1. Business risk: the possibility that the obligations of service will require more resources than available in the contract, particularly fees.
2. Professional liability: the possibility that an error in judgement will result in an assertion of professional negligence in violation of the duty of care.

The business risks of machine intelligence in architecture are more existential, and these are addressed in a later section in this chapter. Of more direct, practical consequence are questions of professional responsibility, duty of care and the implications of machines making complex decisions either in support of (augmentation) or in lieu or (automation) human architects.

TECHNOLOGY AND TECHNICAL RESPONSIBILITY

Despite its admittedly slow pace, broad swathes of the design and construction supply chain are being digitised today with an array of procedural, automation and data management tools. In architecture, BIM is the most prominent of such instruments,[6] but this software falls largely into the category of automating, rather than autonomous, instrumentation. While certain aspects of its functionality are entirely autonomous (such as the generation of schedules and views), BIM relies on minute interactions with a designer to instantiate design data, and the attribution of responsibility for the results of this interaction are unambiguous: the architect using the tool is responsible for its output. This is consistent with the concept of responsible control established by both the ARB[7] and NCARB.[8]

Even in circumstances where the responsible designer relies on technology for substantive portions of technical analysis, there can be no assumption of delegated authority to software or its producers. A vivid example of this relationship is in the allied discipline of structural engineering, where software like Tekla Structures has been used for years for routine calculations of loads and generation of structural details. Repeated use (and professional validation) of this technology has led engineers to rely upon it to produce calculations upon which buildings literally stand, but the engineer of record is still personally liable for that work, irrespective of computer output.

Representational tools like BIM, or analytical tools like structural engineering software, have two important distinctions from their potential AI-enabled successors:

1. A given set of inputs to such software reliably produces a set of results, creating predictability and reliability in the relationship between the two.
2. If necessary, the creators of the underlying software code can explain, with precision, the foundational logic whereby a given input produced a given output, and potential anomalies can be, at least in theory, repeated and, if necessary, diagnosed and corrected.

A future machine learning-based tool, however, has neither of these reassuring characteristics. Given that its underlying code evolves constantly as it is exposed to more data, the algorithm may decide to make different choices at different times, based on the same set of constraints, parameters or inputs. And since deep learning systems in particular are notoriously obscure – as they construct their own internal logics – it will be impossible to determine why a given decision has been made.

Of course, as an architect becomes more experienced, she may also make different decisions about an identical set of circumstances and, as a result, generate different results. The difference, however, is that if she makes an error, we know who to hold responsible. This is hardly the case with software.

THE RESPONSIBILITY OF ALGORITHMS

In fact, the polar opposite is the case. Before you are allowed to access any piece of commercial software, you are required to acknowledge agreement with that software's 'End User License Agreement', or EULA. The EULA explains, in turgid terms, exactly what you can – and cannot – do and expect from the software you have licensed.[9]

My former employer, Autodesk, has millions of users worldwide, including a lot of architects, engineers and contractors. At the risk of either inspiring you to turn the page in boredom or abandon the chapter entirely, I quote at length below two relevant but nonetheless redacted passages from the standard Autodesk EULA, with emphasis (bolding) added. While painful to read, they are illuminating:

5.2 Disclaimer. EXCEPT FOR THE EXPRESS LIMITED WARRANTY PROVIDED
IN SECTION 5.1 (LIMITED WARRANTY), AND TO THE MAXIMUM EXTENT
PERMITTED BY APPLICABLE LAW, **AUTODESK AND ITS SUPPLIERS MAKE,
AND LICENSEE RECEIVES, NO WARRANTIES, REPRESENTATIONS, OR
CONDITIONS OF ANY KIND, EXPRESS OR IMPLIED** (INCLUDING, WITHOUT
LIMITATION, ANY IMPLIED WARRANTIES OF MERCHANTABILITY, FITNESS
FOR A PARTICULAR PURPOSE, OR NONINFRINGEMENT, OR WARRANTIES
OTHERWISE IMPLIED BY STATUTE OR FROM A COURSE OF DEALING
OR USAGE OF TRADE) WITH RESPECT TO ANY AUTODESK MATERIALS,
RELATIONSHIP PROGRAMS, OR SERVICES (PURSUANT TO A RELATIONSHIP
PROGRAM OR OTHERWISE) ... **AUTODESK DOES NOT WARRANT:... THAT
THE OPERATION OR OUTPUT OF THE LICENSED MATERIALS OR SERVICES
WILL BE UNINTERRUPTED, ERROR-FREE, SECURE, ACCURATE, RELIABLE,
OR COMPLETE**, WHETHER OR NOT UNDER A RELATIONSHIP PROGRAM OR
SUPPORT BY AUTODESK OR ANY THIRD PARTY...

6.1 Functionality Limitations. The Licensed Materials and Services ...
are commercial **professional tools intended to be used by trained
professionals only**. Particularly in the case of commercial professional
use, the Licensed Materials and Services **are not a substitute for
Licensee's professional judgment or independent testing**. The Licensed
Materials and Services are intended only to assist Licensee with its design,
analysis, simulation, estimation, testing and/or other activities and are
**not a substitute for Licensee's own independent design, analysis,
simulation, estimation, testing, and/or other activities**, including those
with respect to product stress, safety and utility.[10]

To make absolutely sure the user understands the importance of the
Disclaimer, it is printed IN ALL CAPITAL LETTERS, whereas the section on
Functionality Limitations is in mixed case. If it is not abundantly clear here,
there are two important concepts to which an end user agrees when using
this software. First, you use the software entirely at your own risk, and the
company assumes no responsibility whatsoever for its fitness for purpose,
accuracy or other outputs. This is often hard for licensees to swallow, given
the cost of a software subscription.

Second, as if that is not enough, the EULA specifies that the software is to
be used by trained professionals who will, allegedly, understand its purpose
and functionality. It goes further to explain that use of this tool by such a
professional is no substitute for professional judgement itself. You may have

some powerful digital instruments at your disposal, but the duty of care still obtains – and you are still on the hook. Please make sure to keep your subscription current.

To be fair to my former employers (and their vendor brethren), there is some logic in this contractual deal. While responsible software companies extensively test their products before release,[11] it is simply impossible to anticipate every combination of user interactions and design conditions the software may need to accommodate during its use. In fact, during my time negotiating contracts for an architectural practice, I used similar 'suitability for use' language when clients demanded digital versions of our drawings, as I had no idea what they might do with that data and how they might try to hold my firm responsible for its uncontrolled use. I also required them to rely on the paper versions of same. There is no practical way to predict or manage the resulting liability of unrestricted data in the wild.

The challenge, of course, is that the complexity of data interactions that include user inputs and software outputs is a magnitude of complexity higher when the software is constantly evolving as a machine learning algorithm. History suggests that software vendors will, in response, move further from responsibility with their next generation tools.[12]

FAILURES OF EXECUTION

Failures in the building industry are common, ranging from the more typical broken schedules and blown budgets to infrequent but calamitous disasters like the Grenfell Tower fire in west London. Somewhere in between these extremes lies the responsibility of buildings to be technically, environmentally, socially and contextually appropriate. Surely technology can play an important part in helping building professionals – and especially principal designers such as architects – do a better job with such outcomes. For the purposes of this particular exploration, the question remains about the extent to which the responsibilities of managing the resulting risks of project execution are increased or diminished by AI-driven tools.

Those risks are sketched in Figure 2.2.1, based on Figure 1.6.5, that examines the fundamental risks of failure when AI is enlisted to assist the architect in each of her four fundamental roles during project execution:

ROLE	AUGMENTED BY AI	REPLACEMENT BY AI	PROFESSIONAL RISK OF FAILURE
AGENT OF THE OWNER	DEMONSTRATED DESIGN RESULTS BASED ON LARGE REPRESENTATIVE DATA AND AI-GENERATED CONCLUSIONS	GENERATION OF COMPLETE DESIGN SCHEMES	INCOHERENT, INEPT OR DANGEROUS SOLUTIONS OTHERWISE UNVETTED FOR FIT FOR PURPOSE
LEADER OF THE DESIGN TEAM	COHERENT DISTRIBUTION OF USEFUL INFORMATION TO THE POINT OF WORK	INTEGRATION OF ENGINEERING AND OTHER REPRESENTATIONS OF THE PROJECT AND COORDINATION OF THEIR WORK	MISCOORDINATION LEADING TO TECHNICAL OR OPERATIONAL ERRORS
GUIDE TO THE DESIGN INFORMATION TO THE BUILDER	DESIGN DATA AUGMENTED BY PROCEDURAL INFORMATION FOR ASSEMBLY AND CONSTRUCTION	AUTOMATIC GENERATION OF CONSTRUCTION DOCUMENTATION, BASED ON INFORMATION DEMANDS OF THE BUILDER	MISMATCH OF INFORMATION FIDELITY, DESIGN DECISION ERRORS, UNTIMELY RESPONSES
PROTECTOR OF THE PUBLIC'S HEALTH, SAFETY AND WELFARE	LIFE SAFETY ANALYSIS AND COMPLIANCE EVALUATION	CODE CHECKING AND CERTIFICATION FOR PERMIT	CONSEQUENTIAL DAMAGES OF INJURY AND DEATH

2.2.1:
ROLES AND
PROFESSIONAL
RISK

Consider these risks in the context of the terrible fire at Grenfell Tower in 2017. In that disaster, a small appliance fire on the fourth floor of a residential high-rise spread uncontrolled through the building envelope, and 72 people perished. Components of that envelope had been replaced during a 2015 refurbishment conducted by the building owners and managers and without direct involvement of the original principal designers. In fact, the requirement that every project even involve a principal designer was implemented in 2015, too late to be relevant during the refurbishment project. The Grenfell disaster was a result of a confluence of technical decisions and errors made by a combination of players from the client, design and construction/building supply industries. It may have been the complex interaction of these players that will ultimately be found to be responsible for the inexcusable deaths at Grenfell, although at the time of writing all those players deny any responsibility.[13]

What is clear from this evaluation is that all the responsibilities of building
– and particularly the architect – in execution are correlated to complex
and ambiguous obligations, tasks, dependencies and outcomes that will
be difficult to delegate to machines, and that in order to assure these
important obligations are fulfilled, humans must remain in charge, EULAs
notwithstanding.

POLICY-MAKING

Building well is undeniably a strong public interest and assuring that
buildings are designed and constructed well is a necessary component of
public policy. The building enterprise continues to increase in complexity,
as clearly demonstrated by phenomena as disparate as the climate crisis (at
a global scale) and the Grenfell disaster (at a project scale). Understanding,
managing and optimising the complex characteristics and interactions of
design decisions, construction strategies, building performance, material
characteristics and even market conditions is a task well suited to big data
and AI/ML. Proper responsibility for managing the application of machine
intelligence in the building enterprise could benefit the public if the
relationship between the two is correctly mediated.

Two policy initiatives are suggested by this logic. Given that each of the
responsibilities described in Figure 2.2.1 might be easily characterised as
a 'wicked problem', it makes little sense for the resulting obligations to be
delegated strictly to machines, which will play an important – but not exclusive
– part in solving them. Thus, despite some suggestions to the contrary,[14]
professional licensing requirements and statutes should be strengthened so
that educated, experienced architects and engineers can remain at the centre
of projects and accept responsibility accordingly.

Public policy with regard to the development, deployment and efficacy of
the technologies upon which we are increasingly reliant must catch up, as
much as possible, with the accelerating pace of machine intelligence. Just as
governments establish, control and enforce regulations about medical devices
and medications, air traffic and aircraft safety, and other aspects of public

health, safety and welfare, it must support the creation of standards and certification protocols for systems and algorithms upon which the building industry will rely, including the data trusts that might be repositories for related information. Much like Underwriter Laboratories in the US is legally tasked with certifying the safety of electrical devices, similar structures should be established for digitally empowered design and building.

BUSINESS RISK AND BEYOND

A final note on the business risks of machine intelligence in the design professions, which have been alluded to elsewhere in this text, particularly Chapter 1.5.

In the **short term**, certain firms will likely establish a viable but short-lived competitive advantage by early adoption of AI that will differentiate their services by capabilities or efficiency. As more firms follow their lead, this advantage will disappear.

Over the **long term**, however, architects are likely to face the same questions of disruption and replacement by cognitive automation as other knowledge workers,[15] although the argument above suggests that the timeline of our destruction may be attenuated. Our demise could be largely eliminated, however, by using the capabilities of AI technologies to increase the value of our services – and by implication, of the built environment itself – and to make society more dependent on architects and the machines that assist them, in that order.

2.3 THE DEMAND FOR PROFESSIONALS

>> IF MACHINES CAN REPLACE KNOWLEDGE
WORKERS, DOES THE BUILDING INDUSTRY,
OR SOCIETY WRIT LARGE, REALLY NEED
ARCHITECTS? ONE THESIS SUGGESTS THAT
MUCH OF OUR WORK AS ARCHITECTS — WHO
PURPORTEDLY DESIGN VERY FEW OF THE
WORLD'S BUILDINGS ANYWAY — COULD BE
EASILY AUTOMATED. PERHAPS ARCHITECTURAL
EXPERTISE COULD BE MORE WIDELY
DISTRIBUTED VIA INTELLIGENT MACHINES
RATHER THAN BY A WIDER REACH AND AGENCY
OF ARCHITECTS? ALTERNATIVELY, THOSE
MACHINES AND THEIR INCREASINGLY POTENT
SUCCESSORS COULD BE SEEN AS TOOLS THAT
EMPOWER ARCHITECTS TO TRULY IMPROVE THE
BUILT ENVIRONMENT. <<

When the UK Government's Health and Safety Executive (HSE) enacted the requirement that building projects require a principal designer, it acknowledged that built assets manifest in three distinct phases: planning, execution and use (followed, presumably, by eventual demolition). Before 2015, when the HSE CDM (Construction, Design and Management) regulations went into effect, designers were considered desirable, but not necessary, participants in the delivery process. This is in stark contrast to US law, where any habitable building of significant size must be designed by a licensed architect,[1] and is likely an indication of the political strength of the construction industry in dictating the terms of building delivery.

HSE makes the case for the necessity for architects (as one option) crisply in their regulation, indicating that principal designers must (emphasis added):

» **Plan, manage, monitor and coordinate** health and safety in the pre-construction phase. In doing so they must take account of relevant information (such as an existing health and safety file) that might affect design work carried out both before and after the construction phase has started.

» **Help and advise** the client in bringing together pre-construction information, and provide the information designers and contractors need to carry out their duties.

» Work with any other designers on the project to **eliminate foreseeable health and safety risks** to anyone affected by the work and, where that is not possible, take steps to reduce or control those risks.

» **Ensure that everyone** involved in the pre-construction phase **communicates and cooperates**, coordinating their work wherever required.

» Liaise with the principal contractor, **keeping them informed of any risks** that need to be controlled during the construction phase.[2]

Missing, of course, from this otherwise nifty summary of the need for designers is anything about the quality of the resulting artefact, including its suitability for use, relationship to context, expressive nature, or even environmental or social appropriateness. These are results that clients who hire architects clearly desire, even though they could meet the CDM requirements with any party willing to assume the role of principal designer. Even so, consider whether an intelligent machine in the foreseeable future might 'plan, manage and coordinate health and safety', 'help and advise the client', 'eliminate foreseeable risks' or 'ensure everyone communicates and cooperates'. If these things were even remotely possible, I suspect construction managers, who perform many of the same tasks during their phase of the work, will join architects at the unemployment office. However, is even considering such a future a good idea?

THE PLAN OF WORK

As an architect who practises in the United States, I have always admired the clarity, flexibility and elegance of the RIBA Plan of Work. It evolves over time, changes to reflect delivery and computational realities, and presents clients and collaborators with a very clear definition of both the arc of a project's lifecycle and the architect's possibilities to participate in a project in its entirety. This structure contrasts starkly with its American counterpart, defined by the American Institute of Architects (AIA) as 'Basic Services' in several stolid and largely unhelpfully described phases like 'Schematic Design', which have remained largely unchanged for decades despite the fluid nature of practice, particularly in the digital age.[3]

A comparison of the two structures, derived from Figure 1.5.2, can be seen in Figure 2.3.1, in which I have also diagrammed the subtle but important implications of the Plan of Work: it can be abstracted to understand the work of architects in four 'super-stages':

1. **Project Definition**, comprised of the stages of work necessary to create the overall approach for the project

2. **Technical Development**, where the approach is refined as an engineered and buildable idea, technical insight integrated and detailed information in preparation for construction created

2.3.1:
SUPER-STAGES
OF THE
ARCHITECT'S
SCOPE OF
SERVICE

	PROJECT DEFINITION			TECHNICAL
RIBA	**0** STRATEGIC DEFINITION	**1** PREPARATION & BRIEFING	**2** CONCEPT DESIGN	**3** SPATIAL COORDINATION
AIA	**PD** PRELIMINARY DESIGN, PROGRAMMING		**SD** SCHEMATIC DESIGN	**DD** DESIGN DEVELOPMENT

3.   **Execution**, where the asset is constructed by the contractor
4.   **Use**, when the building is occupied.[4]

In contrast with the 'bottom up' analysis of services we looked at in Chapter 1.5, let us consider the implications of machine intelligence on these super-stages and how the work of the architect might be either augmented or replaced.

PROJECTIVE RESPONSIBILITIES

At the heart of the architect's value in creating the built environment is what I will call, for purposes of this discussion, her 'projective responsibilities' to generate and instantiate ideas about the future state of the building she is designing. To do this job, her conceptual skills must range from broad-scale predictions about the implications of her building in the city, to the minute choices of finishes in the interior; this is a very broad remit, particularly when each of these decisions should support an integrated vision of the project.

Design, as apart from construction, is essentially an Enlightenment era idea about how humans should make things, and was defined for architecture by Leon Battista Alberti around 1450, when he wrote that buildings should be 'conceived in the mind, made up of lines and angles, and perfected in the learned mind and imagination'[5] and then executed without deviation by builders, whose job was to convert the design projection into a built reality.[6] And while it has been argued that architecture has long relied on structured, formalised systems ranging from Vitruvian Orders to off-the-shelf storefront window systems[7] that make for easy pickings by AI, the range of imaginative obligations demanded of today's architects, particularly in the project definition super-phase of the work, defy systematic outputs by algorithms. There is simply too much ambiguity, need for judgement and trade-offs, and demand to solve wicked problems at a variety of scales.

DEVELOPMENT		EXECUTION		USE
4 TECHNICAL DESIGN	NOT USED	5 MANUFACTURING + CONSTRUCTION	6 HANDOVER	7 USE
CD CONSTRUCTION DOCUMENTS	PR PROCUREMENT	CA CONSTRUCTION CONTRACT ADMIN	NOT USED	POE POST OCCUPANCY EVALUATION

Today's AI/ML systems see patterns, particularly those that humans cannot divine, by virtue of the vast ocean of data available to those systems, but they are only projective to the extent they have specific computational templates to follow, like the rules of chess or Go. Their ability to project the future state of, say, a building design, is a function of past experience (as defined by data generated by other projects) and whatever rule set they have been programmed to follow. Completely missing in today's systems is the ability to reason counter-factually or to understand causality (why something did or did not happen) versus correlation (something might happen because, statistically, it has happened under the same circumstances before). Ironically, this argument is made best by computer scientist Judea Pearl, who invented the statistical theory called Bayesian networks, upon which today's correlation-reliant machine learning neural network systems are based.[8]

Pearl is convinced that truly intelligent machines are not possible until they can reason causally and climb what he calls 'The Ladder of Causation' (see Figure 2.3.2), which has three rungs:

Association (where understanding is a function of observing data); Intervention (where actions are possible based on projecting the implications of the future), and Counterfactuals (where understanding leads to ideas based not just on actions but counter-factual assertions about the future). Today's systems are firmly planted on the lowest rung.

The ladder is a sophisticated successor to the theories of Roger Schank, mentioned earlier. Schank believed that the true test of any intelligent machine was the ability to reason inferentially – a different take on Pearl's assertions of Intervention and Counterfactual reasoning. He suggested that the logic of inference was at the heart of human language and cognition. If a machine could draw a conclusion by 'understanding' the logic of implications, it could be said to be reasoning like a human. Unfortunately, this thesis was strongly hobbled by the crude machines we programmed in the 1970s and the need to explicitly code all the resulting cognitive logic. Schank's thesis faded with the 'AI Winter' of the 1980s.

Pearl's ladder is not simply a software roadmap for 21st-century AI systems, but rather yet another assertion about the fundamental nature of human intelligence, one that differentiates humans from other species and accounts for our accelerated progress:

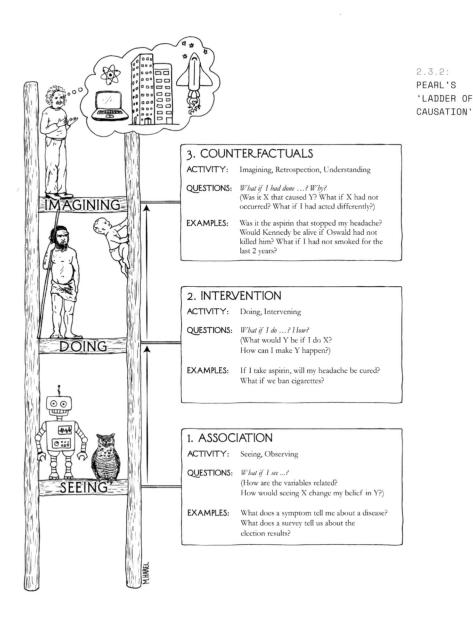

3. COUNTERFACTUALS

ACTIVITY: Imagining, Retrospection, Understanding

QUESTIONS: *What if I had done ...? Why?*
              (Was it X that caused Y? What if X had not
              occurred? What if I had acted differently?)

EXAMPLES: Was it the aspirin that stopped my headache?
              Would Kennedy be alive if Oswald had not
              killed him? What if I had not smoked for the
              last 2 years?

2. INTERVENTION

ACTIVITY: Doing, Intervening

QUESTIONS: *What if I do ...? How?*
              (What would Y be if I do X?
              How can I make Y happen?)

EXAMPLES: If I take aspirin, will my headache be cured?
              What if we ban cigarettes?

1. ASSOCIATION

ACTIVITY: Seeing, Observing

QUESTIONS: *What if I see ...?*
              (How are the variables related?
              How would seeing X change my belief in Y?)

EXAMPLES: What does a symptom tell me about a disease?
              What does a survey tell us about the
              election results?

>> *What humans have that other species lacked was a mental representation of their environment – a representation that they could manipulate at will to imagine hypothetical environments for planning and learning ... (they have) the ability to create and store a mental representation of their environment, interrogate the representation, distort it by mental acts of imagination, and finally ask the 'What if?' kinds of questions.*[9] <<

Pearl speculates that the most important ideas in history were the result of 'wild modelling strategies' (like the Earth astride a giant turtle as early astrophysics) and that algorithms that merely fit data to scenarios could never generate such concepts.[10] 'Imagining hypothetical environments', or, in more prosaic terms, 'Project Definition', is the central value of a good architect and demands third-rung talents that are unlikely to be achieved by machines anytime soon. In fact, should machines reach the second rung, we might achieve tools that help architects speculate on 'what if', the more modern versions of today's analysis software, that could be hugely helpful to the human architects occupying the top of Pearl's ladder.

TECHNICAL COMPRESSION

If the value of projectivity firmly roots human architects in the responsibilities of project definition, our future involvement in technical definition is less clear. Once design strategies have been defined – choosing and spatially coordinating systems, generating coherent and coordinated documents, analysing performance and cost, and organising and transmitting information from designers to builders – are formalised protocols that are more suited to automation. As digital project histories become available as data sources, empiricist systems or even those reaching Pearl's cognitive capabilities of the 'intervention' rung, may assume more responsibility for technical integration. Digitally automated construction and fabrication systems can consume data systematically generated by their AI counterparts on the design side. All of which is to suggest that the technical development super-stage is much more subject to AI replacement than its predecessor in project definition.

However, there is an important caveat here. Health and safety considerations are at the forefront of HSE's requirement for a principal designer, and while AI tools are likely to get much smarter in guiding projects towards safer outcomes, there is little benefit in allocating that responsibility exclusively to algorithms, which are far from being capable of making decisions and therefore taking the corresponding obligations.

As philosopher Daniel C. Dennett suggests, computers are not conscious entities, cannot suffer consequences of failure and do not assume human obligations. He asks if it is possible to 'Give me the specs for a robot that could sign a binding contract – not as a surrogate for some human owner but on its own ... as a morally responsible agent.'[11] If there is any lesson from Grenfell, it is that the complexity of the building enterprise – in all dimensions of design, construction, supply chain management, certification and regulation, and human behaviour – is beyond the ken of machines. As Dennett further posits: 'We don't need conscious agents. There is a surfeit of natural conscious agents, enough to handle whatever tasks should be reserved for such special and privileged entities. We need intelligent tools.'[12]

HEALTH, SAFETY, WELFARE AND THE FUTURE

In summer 2020, academic administrators (like me) were facing the daunting task of planning the upcoming school year in the face of a global pandemic. Under the rubric of 'everything looks like a nail when all you have is a hammer', our team at the School of Architecture began looking for an architectural strategy to address an epidemiological crisis. We knew that if we could translate the spatial demands of public health parameters (established by our colleagues in the School of Public Health) we had a chance of maintaining some semblance of the education our students so reasonably expect. After a summer of careful planning, we produced an operating plan – 50 pages of architectural and engineering analysis – that allowed us to open our building and give our students access to our facilities while working in studio. Every classroom was evaluated and rearranged so those faculty who could teach in person might do so. Air systems were evaluated and adjusted, and a safe occupancy schedule established and enforced. The school year ended without almost no positive cases among our students.

Architects in the 21st century face an array of similar challenges that must draw the profession away from its obsession with making beautiful objects for the wealthy. At the top of this list is climate change, followed closely by housing inequity, structural racism in the built environment, especially cities, even questions of modern slavery in the building supply chain.[13]

In the aggregate, these challenges comprise a new definition of the public's health, safety and welfare, an idea that catalyses the need for a principal designer in the UK and is the basis of professional licensure in the US. Facing these questions as a set of spatial challenges demands the essentially human capabilities of Russell's intuition, insight and intuition that are unlikely to be provided by machines soon, and certainly not in time to attack these problems with the 'wild modelling strategies' they will demand. As Dennett so wisely posits, AI producers should be 'making tools, not colleagues'.[14] Architects are needed as never before, empowered by those tools.

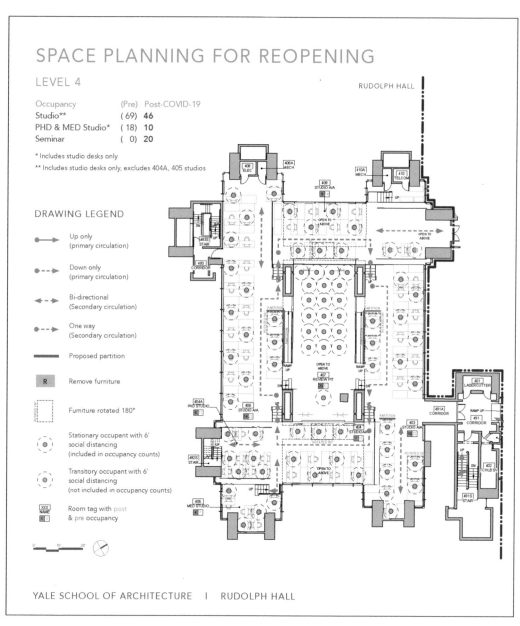

SPACE PLANNING FOR REOPENING

LEVEL 4

RUDOLPH HALL

Occupancy	(Pre)	Post-COVID-19
Studio**	(69)	46
PHD & MED Studio*	(18)	10
Seminar	(0)	20

* Includes studio desks only

** Includes studio desks only, excludes 404A, 405 studios

DRAWING LEGEND

Up only
(primary circulation)

Down only
(primary circulation)

Bi-directional
(Secondary circulation)

One way
(Secondary circulation)

Proposed partition

R   Remove furniture

Furniture rotated 180°

Stationary occupant with 6'
social distancing
(included in occupancy counts)

Transitory occupant with 6'
social distancing
(not included in occupancy counts)

Room tag with post
& pre occupancy

YALE SCHOOL OF ARCHITECTURE   I   RUDOLPH HALL

2.3.3:
YALE
ARCHITECTURE
STUDIO SPACE
PLANNING
(COURTESY
APICELLA
+ BUNTON
ARCHITECTS)

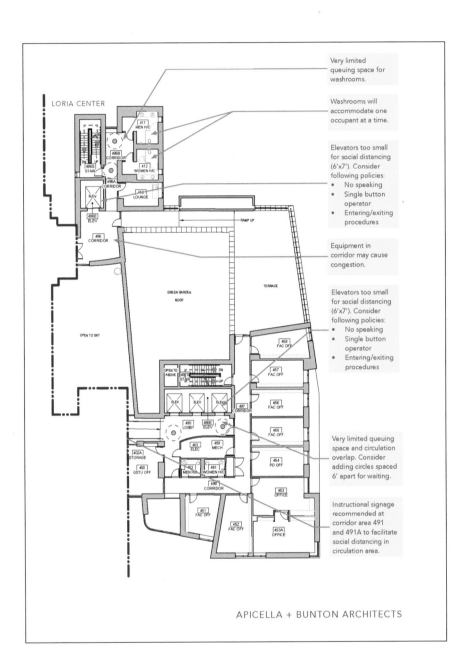

Very limited queuing space for washrooms.

Washrooms will accommodate one occupant at a time.

Elevators too small for social distancing (6'x7'). Consider following policies:
- No speaking
- Single button operator
- Entering/exiting procedures

Equipment in corridor may cause congestion.

Elevators too small for social distancing (6'x7'). Consider following policies:
- No speaking
- Single button operator
- Entering/exiting procedures

Very limited queuing space and circulation overlap. Consider adding circles spaced 6' apart for waiting.

Instructional signage recommended at corridor area 491 and 491A to facilitate social distancing in circulation area.

LORIA CENTER

APICELLA + BUNTON ARCHITECTS

2.4 EDUCATION, CERTIFICATION AND TRAINING

>> TECHNOLOGIES, BY THEMSELVES, RARELY BEND THE ARC OF ARCHITECTURAL EDUCATION OR CERTIFICATION. NEW TOOLS CHANGE THE NATURE OF THE ARCHITECTURAL PROCESS, ALBEIT VERY SLOWLY, AND THE INTELLECTUAL INFRASTRUCTURE OF THE PROFESSION – SCHOOLS, PROFESSIONAL ASSOCIATIONS AND LICENSURE BOARDS – ARE EVEN SLOWER TO RESPOND. THE ADVENT OF INTELLIGENT MACHINES AND THE DEMANDS ON 21ST-CENTURY DESIGN WILL REQUIRE THESE INSTITUTIONS TO RETHINK HOW ARCHITECTS ARE TRAINED, THE CRITERIA BY WHICH THEY ARE CERTIFIED AND THE INTELLECTUAL INFRASTRUCTURE OF THE PROFESSION ITSELF. <<

I have argued to this point that while AI systems are likely to both augment and impinge on the work of architects, they are unlikely to replace us as designers, a capability that will require the development of artificial general intelligence (AGI). The data scientist Herbert Roitblat correlates AGI with just such an ability to attack the 'wicked' problem of design, suggesting that 'To have a truly general intelligence, computers will need the capability to define and structure their own problems,'[1] which is an excellent way to characterise the value of a talented designer.

There are, of course, many problems facing architects in the day-to-day business of design that are well structured and suited to emergent, empiricist machine learning systems. This will be increasingly true as architecture and the scientific disciplines necessary to attack issues of climate change, material performance or even the socio-economic dynamics of building become more entwined. Although data-dependent analytical tools that can help architects with these issues are a far cry from the representational tools like CAD or BIM, which have been treated largely as instruments of expression in both the academy and the office, their emergence suggests that the two poles of intellectual infrastructure of architecture – academic and professional institutions – must plan for the resulting implications.

LEARNING OBJECTIVES

We will touch first on the well-trod and contested ground between those who prepare architects for practice in the academy and those who establish the criteria for accredited curricula and, eventually, professional certification that leads to licensure. The uneasy truce between providers of architectural talent, the certifiers of competence and the consumers of that talent in daily practice is underpinned by a basic tension: what does it mean to educate a competent practitioner? To crudely summarise the positions of the contestants, educators argue that architecture is best understood as a form of culture, and it is difficult, time-consuming and expensive to train students in the design skills necessary to achieve that end, so there is little time to do much else. Licensure certifiers define competency in terms of the legal demands of the public's health, safety and welfare, and demand technical competency first. They are bolstered by professional associations that protect the brand and potency of architects and steer toward capabilities with marketplace relevance. Meanwhile, the practices just want folks who can function the day they first sit down behind their assigned computer.

The means by which these competing aspirations place demands on the architect include:

» curriculum and accreditation constraints (in the academy)
» testing and experience and continuing professional education (by the licensing authorities), and
» qualifications for membership and more continuing education (by professional associations).

While the standards and structures differ slightly, these arrangements are largely the same in the UK and US, and compiled in Figure 2.4.1.

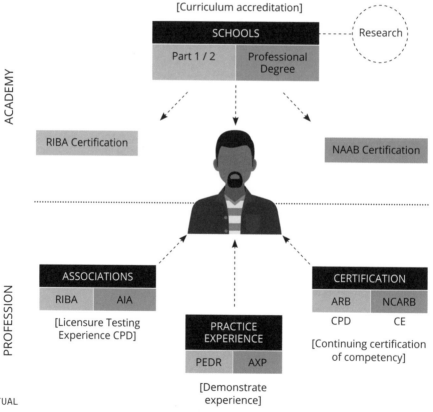

2.4.1:
INTELLECTUAL
DEMANDS
ON THE
ARCHITECT

These competing constituencies, with our architect in the middle, take divergent positions about what constitutes competence and use different instruments to enforce them. The emergence of new technologies, at least to date, has changed these positions little, if it all, since those technologies have largely been technical means (software) to representational ends (drawings, models). However, once computers begin to augment (or replace) competence, the conditions on this pitch will need to change.

TERMS OF TOOLS

The advent of BIM demonstrates this intransigence and holds potential lessons for the upcoming era of AI. As that technology began widespread adoption around 2010, at a point where the software was sufficiently mature, machines capable and when propellants like the UK BIM Mandate came into focus, there was widespread conversation about how a new means of data-rich representation might empower architects and the building industry writ large. Early academic enthusiasm, however, soon faded, and despite massive investments in software and hardware, design pedagogy remained largely unchanged.[2] While BIM is begrudgingly taught in most schools, it is done so as a necessary evil to prepare students for practice, and widespread research on the possible implications of BIM for design pedagogy are somewhat unexplored territory.[3]

I would argue that the disinterest in fully engaging BIM in design curricula is indicative of the larger inclination of educators to see technologies only as tools or instruments, although there are specialised, post-graduate BIM technical degrees for those so inclined.[4] Since BIM joined a crowded field of 'representational' instruments (used directly to depict a design), and that software is deployed largely in the service of form- and image-making, this conclusion is understandable. At my institution we are careful to say that we teach principles and theory, not tools, and there are no parts of the curriculum (save one) where learning tools can result in credit toward the degree.[5]

This arm's-length relationship, however, will not serve either students or the overall professional well in the long term, and the advent of machines that can do knowledge work is best faced now by educators and other leaders of our profession. As intelligent machines move from efficient depiction and data management (CAD, BIM) to analysis, insight and evaluation (AI/ML), the academy must face two parallel obligations:

1. Instantiating a different source of design insight into design pedagogy.
2. Providing the foundational research around the data sources and uses that newly intelligent instruments require.

These two objectives are self-reinforcing; by laying out the proper terms of intelligent digital competence in the enterprise of design, the academy can set the direction for their use in the marketplace.

It is important to draw the distinction here between the development of algorithms that design things themselves and those that provide a supporting role. Subscribing to the earlier argument that we need 'tools, not colleagues',[6] some of the most interesting research today in the architecture/ML nexus looks at what we can learn from algorithmic generation of building plans or room configurations, like that of Stanislas Chaillou of Harvard Graduate School of Design (see Figure 2.4.2).

This work is important in that it may yield insights into building organisation, or even optimisation. It allows designers to see problems in a different light, but it does not solve those same problems. Stuart Russell suggests that '... AI research has focused on systems that are better at making decisions, but that is not the same as making better decisions'.[7] Thus, this research is not likely to be of the most immediate use in a world when structured, scientific and technical interrogation and evaluation of design work will be increasingly demanded.

Finally, recent graduates often introduce new technologies and methods to practice, where technology hesitancy is a function of conservative work processes, long project schedules, costs of implementation and low profit margins. If AI strategies for architecture can be incubated in the academy, perhaps they can be carried into regular practice by the most technologically adept new employees.

PROFESSIONAL PREROGATIVES, CERTIFICATIONS AND DEMANDS

On leaving the academy, our future architect enters the domain of the profession and its disparate masters: registration authorities and professional associations and accreditors, both with roles in certifying competence, and therefore in defining the knowledge and skills that a professional architect must possess. However, where technology once relieved architects of the obligation for such prosaic obligations as consistent hand-lettering and line weights on drawings (that were not of much concern to certifiers), or even

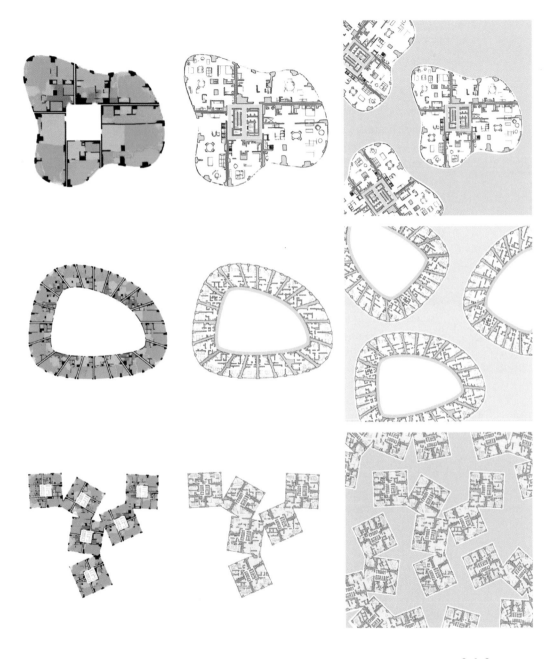

2.4.2:
AI-BASED
PLAN
GENERATION

properly coordinating callouts on CAD drawings, its role in both dispensing and generating knowledge that supports the design process should draw more careful attention.

In the US, the National Council of Architectural Registration Boards is the organisation, comprised of licensure authorities of 54 US jurisdictions, that sets certification standards for architectural registration. As part of their protocols for establishing testing and experience standards, as well as influencing the accreditors of architectural schools, they prepare a 'Practice Analysis of Architecture' to determine what skills practising architects and educators believe are necessary for recent graduates and licensees to master, whether in school or otherwise. Even in 2012, the year the last analysis was completed (see Figure 2.4.3), there was strong agreement that technological skill was necessary to be deemed competent, if only towards various representational ends (like drawings).

2.4.3:
NCARB 2012
PRACTICE
ANALYSIS OF
KNOWLEDGE/
SKILLS
RELATED TO
TECHNOLOGY[8]

While we wait for the 2020 analysis, it is safe to presume that the 2032 analysis will include knowledge and skills of AI applications, and the overall summary of competencies will reflect the idea that certain functions of today's architects, particularly those related to building science, will be performed by machines and managed and integrated into project process by architects.

EDUCATORS

ARCHITECTS

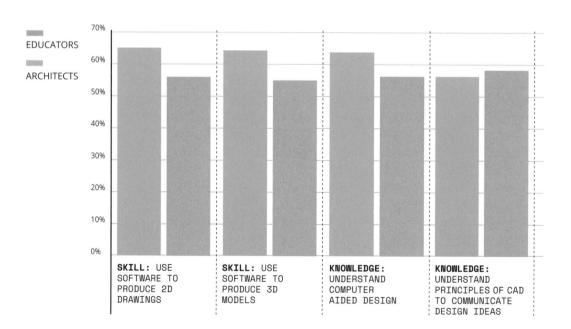

| | SKILL: USE SOFTWARE TO PRODUCE 2D DRAWINGS | SKILL: USE SOFTWARE TO PRODUCE 3D MODELS | KNOWLEDGE: UNDERSTAND COMPUTER AIDED DESIGN | KNOWLEDGE: UNDERSTAND PRINCIPLES OF CAD TO COMMUNICATE DESIGN IDEAS |

The lessons of the UK National Level 2 BIM Standard, which stipulates both the information outputs and performance levels of the design process when powered by BIM, may be instructive.[9] It was created by an industry consortium and eventually evolved from a UK-only template (PAS 1192) to an international standard (ISO 19650). While some practitioners in the UK may avoid working in BIM, any government-funded project requires it for the large number of industry projects they fund, and it is a matter of time before BIM techniques and data strategies will be instantiated into the standard of professional care, expected of competent practitioners.

The Level 2 standard was based on a larger industry strategy established by the Cabinet Office as part of a national economic agenda to improve building and UK construction competitiveness globally, decrease climate impacts of construction and make government building more efficient.[10] The resulting technology requirements were designed to provide process and outputs towards those ends, and acknowledged the importance of information strategies:

>> *Information management using building information modelling can enable dramatic improvement in delivery and performance efficiencies by catalysing increasingly innovative ways of working across the built environment. As an information-based industry, this approach is helping to support better strategic decisions, improved predictability through better risk management and – when coupled with a soft-landings methodology (Annex B of this guidance) – can lead to certainty of operational outcomes and improved learning.[11]* <<

The particular implications for the instruments of professional certifiers – licensing criteria, testing, experience and continuing professional develop – should be derived both organically from emerging practice standards and duties of care, and strategically from cross-industry efforts like Level 2 BIM that set technological objectives and standards of use from agreed goals.

This suggests that the most important role of certifiers in establishing the use of machine intelligence should not stem from determining or driving the particular and unique requirements of AI-supported architectural practice but rather in concert with larger industry collaborators who can prioritise the most important objectives and use of these new systems. This approach will be not just desirable but necessary, given that, unlike BIM tools that generate data by virtue of its use, AI/ML systems require large, well-curated data sets for training and optimisation, and those data are most useful when contributed across the entire delivery chain. The training obligations demanded by certifiers do not serve only as requirements for professionals, but for the machine learning systems as well.

Professional associations, like RIBA or AIA, have more vague ideas about certification for membership, as such considerations are primarily designed to assure that members have credibility with the marketplace. Continuing professional development requirements ask only that member architects be regularly exposed to a broad spectrum of technical and professional concerns, stipulating general categories (such as 'Health, Safety and Welfare', for example, in the US) and numbers of hours of attendance. Over the next decade, as architectural clients rely on AI-based processes in their business or government operations, it is possible that those clients will ask the same of their architects, and professional education and CPD certification are sure to follow the desires of the customer base.

PRESSING PROBLEMS OF INSIGHT

The marketplace is currently pressing the building industry about carbon and climate change, and that challenge gives us a good opportunity to speculate on how the academic and professional platforms of architecture might respond in the time of machine intelligence. Imagine the following scenario:

In 2032 the Ministry of Justice issues a request for proposals for a new headquarters building in Westminster. The project is to adhere to the recent update of ISO 19650, the so called 'Intelligent Level 3 BIM' mandate, and reflect best practices in responsible environmental design, including certifications that the project will be net zero, generate at least 500 construction jobs and be free of any evidence of modern slavery in labour or material practices.

The Construction Industry Council, with participation of RIBA, ARB and a consortium of universities including Cambridge, Liverpool, Manchester and the Architectural Association, has certified a complement of artificial intelligence platforms for the evaluation of embodied carbon and the labour supply chain. Those systems were built, based on research in the consortium, by several companies in the M4 Corridor, the so-called 'England's Silicon Valley', and trained with the National Building Data Trust, created and curated by the Infrastructure and Projects Authority in 2026 with data provided by the UK's global design and construction industry.

The RFP (Request for Proposal) stipulates that submitting architects must be RIBA certified in machine data analytics for Level 3 outcomes, and able to deploy AI platforms to evaluate submitted schemes for compliance to climate, economic and labour performance. The team must also include at least two architects with registrations in the recently approved SPLC (Speciality Professional Licence Certification) created by ARB in climate change modelling and supply chain management evaluation. Several graduate candidates from Leeds and Liverpool have sat for, and received, these special registrations.

The SPLC program has been created in concert with a new definition of Principal Designer established in 2029 by the Health and Safety Executive that includes environmental and labour equity in the responsibilities for that designation. Many firms have been experimenting with two AI platforms, smartTALLY (see Figure 2.4.4) and buildFRDM (see Figure 2.4.5), that assess Level 3 BIM schemes for embodied carbon and forced labour, and collect information about design decisions and strategies that are contributed to the National Building Data Trust. The HSE has further stipulated that projects for human habitation larger than 300 sqm must have an assigned Principal Designer who is a licensed architect, causing some consternation amongst the country's construction/design managers – none of whom have been certified in data-driven design methods.

This admittedly rosy scenario presupposes that our profession organise itself in ways as yet unseen to accomplish three ends:

1. a strategic focus on key social challenges
2. the intelligent deployment of technology in service of that focus
3. the integration of academic, professional and technical resources used in concert toward those ends.

In these circumstances, AI technology is not just an available tool, but more importantly a catalyst of change in standards, relationships and processes, and an opportunity to synchronise education, certification and subsequent professional training in technology suitable for 21st-century design and building.

2.4.4:
TALLY
CARBON BIM
ASSESSMENT
TOOL THAT
EVALUATES
EMBODIED
CARBON IN
BUILDING
MATERIALS
FROM A
DIGITAL
CONCEPTUAL
DESIGN IN
REVIT

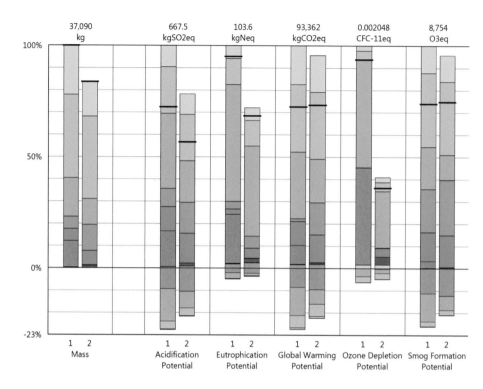

| 37,090 kg | 667.5 kgSO2eq | 103.6 kgNeq | 93,362 kgCO2eq | 0.002048 CFC-11eq | 8,754 O3eq |

| 1 2 | 1 2 | 1 2 | 1 2 | 1 2 | 1 2 |
| Mass | Acidification Potential | Eutrophication Potential | Global Warming Potential | Ozone Depletion Potential | Smog Formation Potential |

Option 1: Corrugated Shingle Cladding

Option 2: Translucent Panel Cladding (selected)

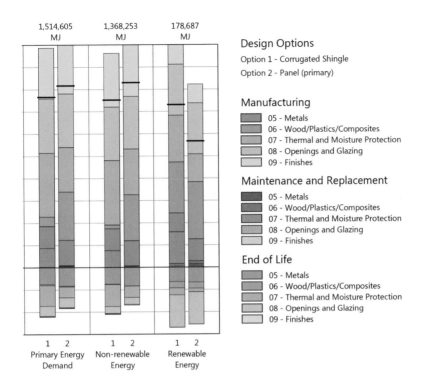

1,514,605 MJ   1,368,253 MJ   178,687 MJ

Design Options

Option 1 - Corrugated Shingle
Option 2 - Panel (primary)

Manufacturing

- 05 - Metals
- 06 - Wood/Plastics/Composites
- 07 - Thermal and Moisture Protection
- 08 - Openings and Glazing
- 09 - Finishes

Maintenance and Replacement

- 05 - Metals
- 06 - Wood/Plastics/Composites
- 07 - Thermal and Moisture Protection
- 08 - Openings and Glazing
- 09 - Finishes

End of Life

- 05 - Metals
- 06 - Wood/Plastics/Composites
- 07 - Thermal and Moisture Protection
- 08 - Openings and Glazing
- 09 - Finishes

| 1 2 | 1 2 | 1 2 |
| Primary Energy Demand | Non-renewable Energy | Renewable Energy |

Results Per Life Cycle Stage, Itemised by CSI Division

2.4.5:
FRDM, AN
AI-BASED
TOOL FOR
FINDING FORCED
LABOUR IN THE
MANUFACTURING
SUPPLY CHAIN

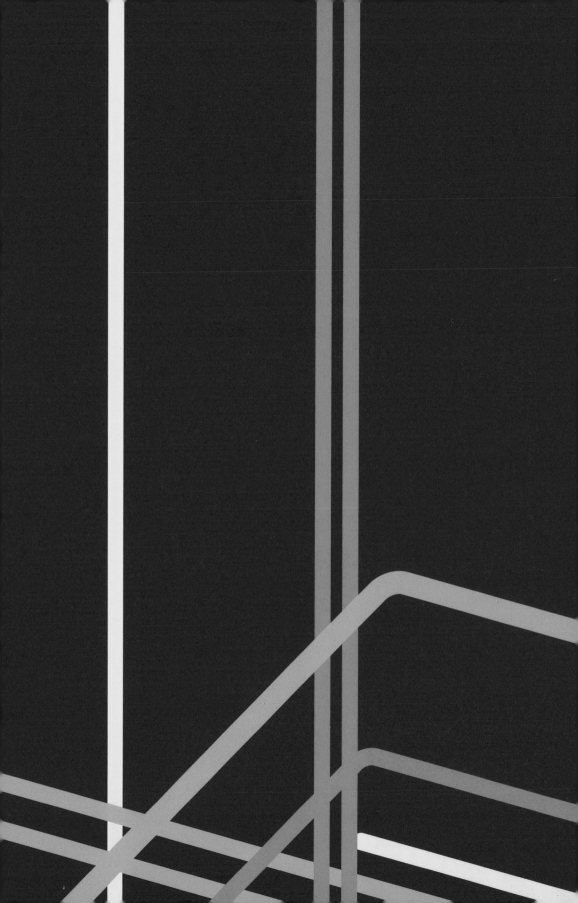

03
RESULTS

>> JUST AS ACCELERATING STORAGE AND PROCESSING
CAPABILITIES OF TODAY'S COMPUTERS HAVE VIVIFIED
MACHINE INTELLIGENCE, THOSE CAPABILITIES IN TURN
BRING THE POTENTIAL OF EXPONENTIALLY MORE PRECISE
AND INSIGHTFUL PROTOCOLS TO DESIGN, SUGGESTING THAT
COMPUTERS (AND, ONE HOPES, THEIR HUMAN MASTERS) MAY
BECOME MUCH MORE SKILLED AT NOT JUST PROJECTING THE
FUTURE STATE OF A BUILDING, BUT IN PREDICTING ITS
BEHAVIOUR. <<

3.1 THE OBJECTIVES OF DESIGN

>> THE INEVITABLE ADDITION OF ARTIFICIAL INTELLIGENCE TOOLS AND 'BIG DATA' IN THE BUILDING INDUSTRY WILL CHALLENGE TOMORROW'S ARCHITECTS TO RE-EXAMINE THE CLASSICAL DEFINITION OF THEIR OBLIGATION TO DEFINE THE 'DESIGN INTENT' OF A PROJECT. AT THIS STAGE, ARCHITECTS LEAVE MANY OF THE IMPLICATIONS OF THEIR IDEAS — FOR CONSTRUCTION AND EVENTUALLY BUILDING OPERATIONS — TO BE RESOLVED AND REFINED BY OTHERS. AI TOOLS ARE LIKELY TO ACCELERATE THE USE OF DATA-DRIVEN EVIDENCE TO AUGMENT THE PRECISION OF DESIGN, GIVE ARCHITECTS GREATER UNDERSTANDING OF PROJECT PERFORMANCE ACROSS THE MANY DIMENSIONS OF PROJECT DELIVERY AND RAISE EXPECTATIONS OF THE RESULTS. THE PROFESSION CAN DECIDE TO SEE THESE OPPORTUNITIES AS AN ADVANTAGE OR A THREAT TO ITS AGENCY. <<

When Alberti defined the architect's design of a building as 'conceived in the mind, made up of lines and angles, and perfected in the learned mind and imagination',[1] he centred those responsibilities on the abstract projection of a future state, which, according to Carpo, was to be translated from idea to concrete result by virtue of the architect's 'sound advice and clear drawings'.[2] Carpo, channelling Alberti, further explains:

>> Designers first need drawings and models to explore, nurture and develop the idea of the building ... (those) models should also be used to consult experts and seek their advice; as revisions, corrections and new versions accumulate, the design changed over time; the whole project must be examined and re-examined... The final and definitive version is attained only when each part has been so thoroughly examined that any further addition, subtraction or change could only be for the worse.[3] <<

In Carpo's interpretation we find three important architectural strategies:

1. The use of abstraction, in the form of models and drawings, to memorialise ideas.
2. The incorporation of outside expertise in completing the design so it is suitable for construction.
3. Designing in successive iterations to refine the project until it could not possibly be adjusted for the better.[4]

Today's architects use much the same approach, bolstered by various digital armaments, but what happens when those tools become agents of design?

THE AI-ENABLED DESIGNER

Let us assume that an architect by, say, the year 2030 has a complement of AI-enabled tools at her disposal, along with significant advancements in the resolution, precision and flexibility of modelling platforms that one hopes would be the logical successors of today's BIM. While there may be a conceptual breakthrough, some time in the future, in what I have described as 'cognitive' AI platforms that can reason inferentially about the complex interactions that comprise a building, let us assume that by 2030 we only are at the point of useful architectural versions of 'undeniably single-mindedly successful'[5] platforms like today's language and game-playing software, for example GPT-3 or AlphaGo.[6] Such systems would be tightly tied to design modelling/representational platforms and their data, and receive training from other information sources like engineering systems, real-world data collection about context from LIDAR or GIS, construction management sources that describe process and results from contractors, and building operations data from existing projects controlled by sensor-driven building management and control systems. These systems are likely to be semi-autonomous, cloud-based agents that operate in the background of the architect's process, appearing when the architect demands some piece of insight or analysis.

While it is impossible to accurately predict what will comprise this new set of AI-empowered tools, Table 3.1.1 summarises a few speculative suggestions designed to sketch the potential future of autonomous, AI-based tools.

Notably absent from this list, save perhaps the last item, are systems tasked with generating entire design solutions (at any scale) for a project. A central thesis of this book is that such systems will not be useful until far in the future – if at all. They are unlikely to provide useful insights and present an unnecessary existential threat to architects. The world is already populated with many not-quite or barely competent buildings; the creation of a design generator capable of even simple buildings is likely to have unintended and unpleasant consequences for the profession. And with so many other opportunities, energies are best focused elsewhere – augmenting the design process to improve the performance and results of design and building.[7]

THREE NEW DIMENSIONS OF DESIGN

These AI examples suggest that Alberti's components of the design process – representation, iteration and expertise – will be transformed as intelligent systems that augment (but do not replace) the central role of the designer. First, as has already been seen in our now data-rich world, the extensive availability of information in digital form, combined with the predictive and analytical power of AI systems, will make the role of **evidence** in supporting design decisions much more apparent. While, as I have argued previously, the credibility of design decisions stemmed primarily from the (presumably) sound judgement and intuition of an experienced architect,[8] those judgements will need to be substantiated, at least in part, by evidence and analysis to back them up. The built environment has traditionally disgorged a collection of ambiguous, heterogenous data sets, but the ability of AI systems to divine and understand patterns within it gives architects the opportunity to

AI-BASED TOOL	CAPABILITY	TRAINING DATA
ZONING AND PLANNING ANALYSER	EVALUATES CONFORMANCE TO SPECIFIC PLANNING AND ZONING CONSTRAINTS OF THE PROJECT	PLANNING CODE, RECORD OF VARIANCES, EXISTING BUILDINGS IN SIMILAR JURISDICTIONS
BUILDING CODE EVALUATOR	CHECKS EMERGING SCHEME FOR CONFORMANCE TO BUILDING/LIFE SAFETY PERFORMANCE	STANDARD CODES AND LOCAL IMPLEMENTATION, EXAMPLES OF CONFORMING CONFIGURATIONS FROM OTHER PROJECTS
SPATIAL COORDINATOR	CHECKS 3D COORDINATION OF BUILDING ELEMENTS WITH AN UNDERSTANDING OF WHEN CONFLICTS ARE PROBLEMATIC	CLASH ANALYSIS OF CURRENT DESIGN SCHEME AND EXAMPLES FROM OTHER PROJECTS OF APPROPRIATE AND PROBLEMATIC INTERFERENCES IN PLENUMS AND OTHER SPACES
CARBON IMPACT CALCULATOR	COMPUTES GENERATED AND EMBODIED CARBON IN THE DESIGN	ENERGY AND CARBON CALCULATIONS AND STANDARDS, RECORDS FROM OTHER PROJECTS, SUPPLY CHAIN AND MATERIAL DATABASES
MEANS AND METHODS EVALUATOR	EXAMINES THE CONSTRUCTABILITY/SEQUENCING AND PROCEDURES NECESSARY TO CONSTRUCT A GIVEN BUILDING ELEMENT TO TEST ITS VIABILITY DURING DESIGN	CONSTRUCTION PROCEDURE INFORMATION FROM BUILDERS AND PRODUCT SYSTEM MANUFACTURERS, CONSTRUCTION SIMULATION AIS.
PRODUCT RECOMMENDATIONS AND SPECIFICATION GENERATOR	EXAMINES CHARACTERISTICS AND RECOMMENDS POSSIBLE MATERIALS AND PRODUCTS AND COORDINATES THE NECESSARY SPECIFICATIONS	PAST PROJECT RECORDS, MATERIAL AND SPECIFICATION DATABASES, PRODUCT MANUFACTURING INFORMATION, SUPPLY CHAIN AVAILABILITY DATA
COST MONITOR	AT THE PROPER LEVEL OF RESOLUTION[9] PROJECTS THE COST OF CONSTRUCTION AND OPERATION	CONSTRUCTION COST DATA FROM PROVIDERS AND PAST PROJECTS; BUILDING OPERATIONS DATA FROM EXISTING PROJECTS
SUPPLY CHAIN AVAILABILITY PROBE	WORKING WITH THE PRODUCT RECOMMENDER, EVALUATES THE SUPPLY CHAIN CONSTRAINTS OF A PRODUCT SELECTION, INCLUDING AVAILABILITY, COST AND FORCED LABOUR ISSUES.	MANUFACTURING AND SUPPLY STREAM SHIPPING AND MANIFESTS, CERTIFICATION DATA, LABOUR STANDARDS INPUTS FROM LOCAL CONDITIONS, MODELS OF PAST PROJECTS
SKETCH PROBLEM SOLVER	BASED ON PARAMETERS SET BY THE DESIGNER, GENERATES ALTERNATIVES FOR A GIVEN DESIGN PROBLEM AND PROVIDES MEASURES OF PERFORMANCE AND SUITABLE FIT FOR PURPOSE	EXAMPLES OF SIMILAR CIRCUMSTANCES IN DESIGN MODELS OR EXISTING BUILDINGS

3.1.1:
FUTURE
AI-BASED
TOOLS

generate and leverage just such evidence. And since many of today's clients rely on AI data systems to run their enterprises, architects will be expected to do the same to substantiate the decisions that form the design.

Alberti has asserted that the architect should produce designs that are perfectly ready for a builder to enact physically. At the end of the design process, Carpo interprets that:

> >> *This is when all revisions and the final blueprint (as we would have said until recently, both literally and figuratively) is handed over to the builders. Thenceforth, no more changes may occur. The designer is no longer allowed to change his mind, and builders are not expected to have opinions on design matters. They must build the building as is – as it was designed and notated.*[10] <<

The master builder of Brunelleschi's ilk, a central repository of all things design and construction and the maker of every decision, gives way to the architect, generator of complete, immutable and clearly depicted ideas.

If only. There is a profound mismatch between Enlightenment aspiration and the realities of modern construction, where design documents are a frequent source of contention and the architect is relegated as a subconsultant of a contractor in the name of better control, while the builder has not just opinions about design, but control over it. However, the advent of AI gives architects an interesting opportunity to close this gap and realise design ideas with great fidelity, if not greater control, of the design-build relationship.

If architects will benefit from AI systems focused on specific tasks, it is equally likely that our colleagues in construction will see similar progress, with AI-driven systems **automating aspects of construction** in the field through robotics and industrialised methods of digitally driven mechanisms. An AI that plays brilliant chess can likely be repurposed to control a robot that installs curtain walls, for example. In doing so, the procedural knowledge of building that architects are oft accused of lacking will have been instantiated digitally and will be accessible to them as an evaluative/performative measure of the efficacy of their design.[11] While sharing the 'mind and imagination' with an AI, the architect can perfect the design with substantial new, accessible understanding of how it can be built.

Finally, deploying evidence in combination with the predictive powers of AI systems will make **performance** a profound objective of the modern design process and its deliverables. Architects today operate in a mode that might be characterised as 'implicit' performance: our work process is organised and calibrated to produce physical artefacts (drawings) that lead to an object (a building) that is hoped to achieve certain ends once complete, and those goals are rarely explicitly defined as measurable objectives or outcomes. Implicit in the design process are expectations that those goals will be achieved, costs will be met, documents completed on schedule, materials properly specified and codes conformed. At the same time, the resulting buildings consume resources and produce carbon, require regular maintenance and staffing, organise the circulation of people and materials, and most importantly create platforms for their owner's objectives: students learning, patients healing, goods selling. They contribute (or detract from) the environment, economic health and social fabric of their locales. As AI systems learn from the data derived from the built environment, and to the extent that these characteristics model in predictive AI systems, architects get the ability to 'explicitly' design projects towards improved ends, demonstrating *a priori*, by virtue of the resulting simulations, that such outcomes are the result of the design itself. And while the earliest opportunities may be of a more limited technical nature (as suggested in Table 3.1.1), more sophisticated systems will model and evaluate larger, more complex contexts.

This power of prediction is perhaps the most important implication of AI for the design process. It seems likely that AI technology, and the building industry data necessary to train it, will be in great supply by 2030. Prediction, according to a recent analysis of AI implementation in business, 'takes information you have, often called "data", and uses it to generate information you don't have'.[12] 'Information you don't have' might be the watchword of today's building industry.

BREAKING FROM ALBERTI'S DESIGN PROTOCOLS

Alberti's design protocols of representation, iteration and instantiation of expertise have not been dramatically transfigured by the first few waves of technology, including even BIM. Representation is still centred on creation of drawings, and while much of the resulting information is now digital, the means by which it is generated – by an iterative refinement informed by outside expert consultants – is today exactly as asserted *c.* 1450. The third wave of digital tools, those driven by intelligent computation, will follow, but dramatically break from these traditions.

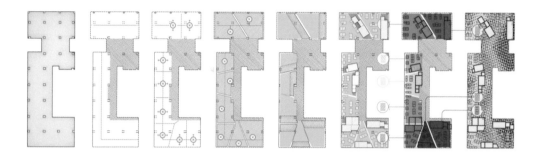

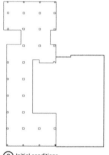

0 Initial conditions.

1 Definition of fixed / non-generative zones and central spine for organizing neighborhoods.

2 A variable number of neighborhoods are seeded along spine, and given a parameterized range of motion.

3 Optimization algorithms shift seeds along the spine creating angular divisions.

4 One edge from each neighborhood is selected to generate zone for amenity clusters.

5 Automated "test fit" generates amenity rooms from space matrix and desk layout.

6 Teams are assigned by best-fit algorithm. Neighborhood amenities are assigned by team preferences.

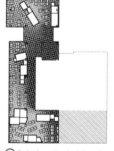

7 Evaluation engine simulates and scores each design, and returns results to genetic algorithm.

3.1.2:
AI-SUPPORTED
STRATEGY
FOR GENERATING
OFFICE
LAYOUTS

AI-enabled representation will stretch the definition of 'model', which once referred to a scaled physical artefact (maquette), a mathematical simulation of geometry (CAD) or a parametric, meta-data-infused simulation of building components in three dimensions (BIM). An AI evaluation of a design will be a predictive model that will substantiate design decisions that are represented by more traditional means, but at the same time it will expand the range of the architect's instruments of service. Those AI models will be required for both validation and as contributions to larger data repositories that can further train other AIs.

An architect I once worked with compared the current iteration process of design to a circular staircase. Looking straight down on it, you appear to be going around in circles, but with each cycle you rise slowly toward the goal. In today's design environment, climbing those process steps is accelerated by the inherent flexibility and accessibility of digital models and enhanced by emergent strategies called generative design, where computerised scripts generate alternatives by varying specific characteristics of a scheme. Properly constrained – so as to not lead to the 'systematic generation of useless alternatives' as César Pelli once described the misuse of CAD – AI-enabled generative design will set its own constraints. It will be informed by the logic of previously approved schemes as a training set and simultaneously provide evaluation of its own results. Design exploration will still demand choices by humans to make decisions that solve 'wicked' problems, but the process will be much more intelligent and systematic.

Generative strategies that connect representation, iteration and instantiation may be the most important implication of AI-supported design processes of the future. Today's modelling and analysis tools can only episodically optimise limited parameters of a design challenge – adjusting the dimensions of a solar shade to limit exposure and thereby reduce the size of a cooling system, for example – but this is hardly a strategy for the complete design of the building enclosure. Over time, AI systems will be able to manage multiple variables while evaluating design representations created by the architects and engineers, instantiating expertise while simultaneously recommending alternative solutions that meet design objectives. As designers select solutions, these systems will come to learn which combined strategies are best, and thereby improve their performance – and that of their architect masters.

Consider the case of an architect coordinating the design of a mechanical/electrical room (MER) in her project. That room, never big enough to satisfy the engineers who fill it with complex equipment and connections, must be integrated in 3D with the balance of the project. She must assure the systems all fit, there is sufficient room for servicing the equipment, and that none of the architecture, structure, lighting and fire suppression interferes with the locations and pathways of the systems. An intelligent AI, trained on many similar rooms and the components that often fill them, can do more than just check the MER layout for clashes (a common feature of today's BIM) but identify potential operational problems, recommend potential configurations, even strategise how to sequence and install the systems. Rapid simulation and evaluation of these issues will speed the process and make a successful solution more likely, improving over time as the AI systems 'learn' what is best. Our architect can use the additional time made available to resolve the proportions of the facade.

Early AI efforts in the 1980s purported to create 'expert systems' that would memorialise knowledge and insight of humans in computer code. Neither the theory nor the technology were up to the task. By contrast, in our AI-enabled design future, sources of expertise that are today provided almost exclusively by human consultants will be greatly expanded by the analytical insights that computers can provide. While conceptual decisions that are more strategic in nature are best dispensed by human experts who can evaluate systems approaches and large-scale choices, specific outputs can be provided for specific tasks with particular inputs that result from well-understood rules. In the examples above, evaluating the particulars of life safety code compliance (and, with it, the arrangement of fire sprinklers or rated corridors) might have been provided by consultant with that expertise. Our designer of the future will apply an AI overlay to her design to yield much the same results, faster, and allowing for further iterations and resolution of the scheme in real time. Her decisions will be catalogued by the assisting AI and guide successive work.

NEW OBJECTIVES, NEW OUTPUTS

At the heart of the potential future changes in the objectives of the design process wrought by AI lie the implications of data and its use. Today's architects use digital tools to create data, translate it into various forms like drawings or specifications, and dispense it as evidence of their design decisions. When machines can consume, create and deploy data to assist in those decisions, the models they create extend to and are entwined with the descriptors of the design itself. The resulting capabilities can make the results of design more precise, transparent and predictable. The balance of this section will explore strategies for enabling these capabilities in ways that further empower architects accordingly.

3.1.3:
MECHANICAL
INFRA-
STRUCTURE
MODELLED IN
BIM FOR A
MODERN
HOSPITAL

3.2 CREATING, CONSUMING AND CURATING DATA

>> DIGITISATION OF THE BUILDING INDUSTRY MAKES DATA MORE PORTABLE, TRANSMITTABLE AND, TO SOME DEGREE, FUNGIBLE. AI SYSTEMS WILL REQUIRE LARGE SWATHES OF SUCH DATA, FIRST FOR TRAINING AND THEN TO PERFORM. A GIVEN PROJECT GENERATES DATA IN A WIDE VARIETY OF FORMATS, SCALES AND LEVELS OF RESOLUTION BY DISPARATE PLAYERS WITH A VARIETY OF MOTIVATIONS TO SHARE IT, OR NOT.
AS AI CHANGES THE DEMAND FOR AND CONSUMPTION OF DIGITAL INFORMATION BY ARCHITECTS, HOW DOES THAT CHANGE THEIR RESPONSIBILITIES AND PROCESS? <<

 In 1994, my former employers at Autodesk organised about a dozen companies across the AECO industry in an effort to address a growing concern. The company's increasingly ubiquitous CAD platform, AutoCAD©, was becoming the data standard for the building industry with their proprietary file format, .DWG. At the same time, the company was building a global ecosystem of third-party developers to create additional functionality on top of the AutoCAD© platform, and other software companies were looking to consume AutoCAD© DWGs in their own systems. The file format itself was understandably defended zealously by Autodesk, as much of their intellectual property was contained in each file.

The 12 companies, including architects, mechanical equipment manufacturers, engineers and at least one real estate developer, called their consortium the 'International Alliance for Interoperability', and opened it to all members by 1995.[1] Their mission was to achieve the ability to seamlessly move data between applications without translation or the need to duplicate DWG functionality. Rebranded BuildingSMART in 2005, the global consortium writes and distributes a data standard called Industry Foundation Classes (IFCs), an attempt to create a common denominator exchange that can transport relevant data between any software that has been written to generate or consume it. BuildingSMART's efforts have turned from CAD data (DWG) to BIM in past years,[2] creating standard data exchanges and libraries designed to make BIM more open.

Achieving interoperability standards in the building industry, even given BuildingSMART's admirable global efforts, is a daunting task. By the late 1990s, DWG had become the standard of data exchange in design and construction powered by two divergent realities: the industry was turning to digital tools, primarily AutoCAD©, but even more importantly, the vector of information exchange for architects and engineers was still largely drawings, rather than more robust data. This made the transmission of information via IFC relatively simple, using common definitions of geometry, lightly dusted with meta-data about that geometry. Given the explosion of digital tools today, the problem, however, is much more complex, and accepted non-proprietary data standards for the AECO industry have not been established.[3]

MORE SOFTWARE, MORE DATA, LESS COOPERATION

The move to BIM was but one part of the inevitable digitisation of AECO writ large. Building things is an information-rich enterprise, and architects among others had to wait until machines and networks were sufficiently powerful to handle the required data. Cloud computing, high-speed interconnectivity and capable mobile devices all have spurred a veritable explosion in digital tools, formats, processes and even hardware.[4] Standards for building information, analogue or otherwise, vary widely from country to country. This makes the mission of BuildingSMART even more challenging, despite their new branding as enablers of the 'full benefits from digital ways of working in the built asset industry'.[5]

However, what became apparent as architects and their collaborations began using larger collections of digital tools was that data exchange and relationships were not just a function of technical standards. Each constituent of the building process has its own contract and risk models, tools, data expectations, representational schema, content and business expectations, and is digitising at its own pace and in its own terms.

In 2004, the US National Institute of Standards and Technology published a report purporting to identify an annual cost of $15.8 billion lost to software interoperability in the capital projects industry. The report gained significant notoriety, and certainly brought attention to the process inefficiencies of non-interoperability among software used for building. It failed, however, to address the underlying structural questions in the industry – discontinuity in business models, disaggregation in the supply chain, conflicting risk management strategies and lack of optimisation incentives in project delivery – that plague construction,[6] all of which are strong disincentives to work together with data.

Those same challenges of cooperation and integration can be seen more broadly in the structure and use of data in the building industry, and especially for architects. Being careful not to create too much responsibility or risk for construction, while managing limited fees with which to produce information, design data is held closely when released at all. Other 'learned' professions carefully generate, curate and consume knowledge about their disciplines: databases of case law, medical research about treatments and outcomes or pharmaceutical efficacy. An attorney researching the legal precedents for her client can explore a complete, cross-referenced database of every relevant legal decision in the history of jurisprudence (see Figure 1.3.3). Architects have access to no such central data. The move towards interoperability was a plea to play nicely together, but not to share any toys.

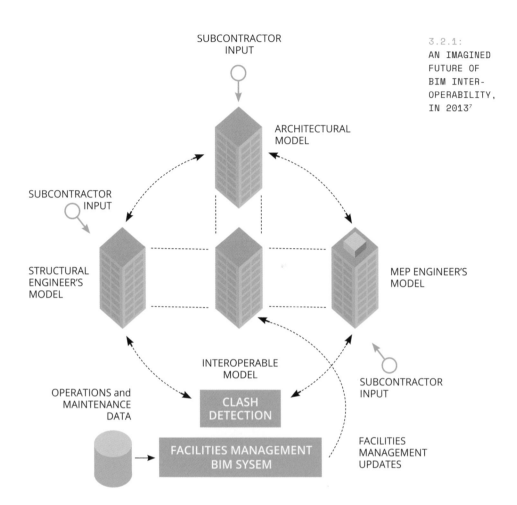

SUBCONTRACTOR
INPUT

3.2.1:
AN IMAGINED
FUTURE OF
BIM INTER-
OPERABILITY,
IN 2013[7]

ARCHITECTURAL
MODEL

SUBCONTRACTOR
INPUT

STRUCTURAL
ENGINEER'S
MODEL

MEP ENGINEER'S
MODEL

INTEROPERABLE
MODEL

SUBCONTRACTOR
INPUT

OPERATIONS and
MAINTENANCE
DATA

CLASH
DETECTION

FACILITIES MANAGEMENT
BIM SYSEM

FACILITIES
MANAGEMENT
UPDATES

3.2.2:
COMPONENTS
OF A
POTENTIAL
DATA TRUST
FOR THE
BUILDING
INDUSTRY

PRECONDITIONS OF INTEROPERABLE DATA

The advent of machine learning-based AI systems demands that our industry not just share toys but builds a new sandbox in which to play with them. This is the first and most important precondition of moving towards and taking complete advantage of the power of AI for architects and other players in the building enterprise. The ability to leverage the potential of AI lies in the profession working closely with industry partners who might also benefit, and sharing data to do so in responsible ways.

The problem, of course, is the other external factors, not the least being underlying motivations (or lack thereof) to share data. We will address some of the structural risk and reward questions in Chapter 3.5, but for purposes of this discussion the issue is diagrammed in Figure 3.2.2, which represents four hypothetical architectural projects that are otherwise unrelated. While there is some motivation to allow the project data generated within your office to roam more freely in the domain of the project, there is no structure nor incentive to organise or share it beyond that limited use.

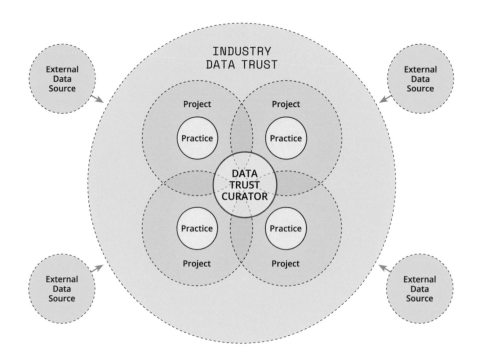

At the centre of the diagram is a proposal to address this issue, which must be solved in order for AI to have any real chance of adoption or use in architecture or the allied building disciplines: a cross-industry data trust that would be the steward of a global building industry information resources. The concept of data trusts has evolved in the last several years to address questions of information coherence, privacy and fiduciary responsibility in circumstances where individuals contribute their personal data that is then used, for commercial purposes, by third parties. A data trust is an independent, third party who collects, manages, anonymises and provides access to such a large-scale collection of data:

> > *Typical use cases for data sharing are fraud detection in financial services, getting greater speed and visibility across supply chains, improving product development and customer experience, and combining genetics, insurance data, and patient data to develop new digital health solutions and insights. Indeed, the research has shown that 66% of companies across all industries are willing to share data. Nevertheless, sharing sensitive company data, particularly personal customer data, is subject to strict regulatory oversight and prone to significant financial and reputational risks.[8] <<*

While it is unlikely that 66% of architects, or contractors for that matter, would be willing to share data today, the benefits of access to a central global repository of project data, properly anaesthetised for attribution, would be too great to pass up, as both a useful reference tool and the necessary information infrastructure to begin AI in earnest. And of course, the challenges presented by European data sharing standards must be overcome.

Such a data trust would, by necessity, need to be cross-disciplinary and include information from designers, builders, subcontractors, product manufacturers and suppliers, and operating building owners; the entire supply chain that builds assets. For architects, there is marginal utility in an 'architecture only' data set, as it is likely to be sparse and inconsistently curated. And if my experience of years as a technology vendor is any indication, most architects are highly sceptical – and unwilling to pay for – new, disruptive technologies, especially in comparison with their colleagues in the building supply chain – engineers, contractors, subcontractors. The architecture business is small, relatively unprofitable and generally unwilling to invest in disruptive technologies, creating a classic chicken-and-egg dilemma in establishing the necessary foundations of artificial intelligence.

Thus cross-industry cooperation is necessary for both data assembly and AI platforms. With the exception of the decision by Autodesk to invest, initially, $133 million in Revit and then develop that platform first for architects, there has been scant history in the technology of major investment in new software or platforms for architects, per se. So while there might be short-term comfort in the idea that perhaps it is too expensive to invest in AI that would replace architects as individual contributors, there is clearly benefit in data sources and AI platforms suited for the entire industry and it is more likely that investment will be made by vendors to address a broader market of customers.

BUILDING AND USING TRUSTABLE DATA

So let us assume that some combination of industry inspiration, government support and academic research has yielded, in our imaginary AI year of 2030, a global building industry data trust where firms are paid to contribute data,

3.2.3:
PROJECT DATA
FLOWS AND
THE DATA
TRUST

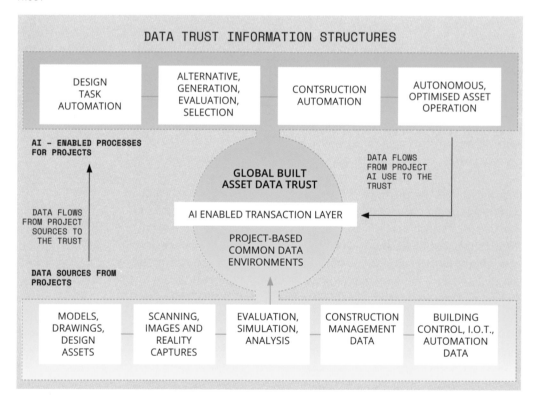

DATA TRUST INFORMATION STRUCTURES

DESIGN TASK AUTOMATION

ALTERNATIVE, GENERATION, EVALUATION, SELECTION

CONTSRUCTION AUTOMATION

AUTONOMOUS, OPTIMISED ASSET OPERATION

AI – ENABLED PROCESSES FOR PROJECTS

GLOBAL BUILT ASSET DATA TRUST

DATA FLOWS FROM PROJECT AI USE TO THE TRUST

AI ENABLED TRANSACTION LAYER

DATA FLOWS FROM PROJECT SOURCES TO THE TRUST

PROJECT-BASED COMMON DATA ENVIRONMENTS

DATA SOURCES FROM PROJECTS

MODELS, DRAWINGS, DESIGN ASSETS

SCANNING, IMAGES AND REALITY CAPTURES

EVALUATION, SIMULATION, ANALYSIS

CONSTRUCTION MANAGEMENT DATA

BUILDING CONTROL, I.O.T., AUTOMATION DATA

and in exchange have access to that data and the AIs that have been trained to use it. Let us further assume that there is enough useful data in the trust that it begins to enjoy widespread adoption and grows with each significant project designed or built, worldwide. Designers, builders, their supply chain and building owners all contribute data that results from their work.

This new relationship is described in Figure 3.2.3, an elaboration of Figure 1.4.2.

The data sources created by a project team, including data from modelling, analysis and other artefacts of architectural design, would be contributed to the data trust. Assuming that its use has become widespread, we might expect some standardisation of software, but I suspect the continued explosion of tools that will result from the widespread digitisation of the industry will make this challenging. It is more likely that AI itself may provide the means to standardise and conform project data from architects and others before it is contributed to the common cause.

Training an AI to recognise a representation of, say, a window in a BIM model, purchase order or shop drawing (if such a thing exists in the future) across those data sets is a question of pattern matching – something machine learning systems do well. One imagines an AI-based 'transaction layer' shown in the diagram, which would collect, translate and standardise project data into consistent relationships and formats, and would be an excellent opportunity for supervised learning, combined with BIM and other evolving model typologies, for next-generation AI platforms. And if such a capability could evolve, it would also improve the project-based common data environments used by individual architects, creating integrated representations of a project before that data streamed, at the appropriate point, into the data trust itself.

An architect would therefore access and consume information, in this construct, in three ways:

1. At the level of the **individual project**, as a result of the development of the design.
2. From the **data trust**, for both reference and to deploy AI-assisted tools (like, for example, the cost estimating and analysis tools described earlier).
3. From **outside data sources** that can inform the development of the design, like economic models of the project context, weather data or information about the availability of site utilities.

DESIGN CREDIBILITY

When structural engineers began to rely on software for routine calculations, the credibility of those results relied not so much on the regulation of or promises by the technology vendors but rather on that the engineer herself was responsible for the output of those systems and any errors that might occur as a result of their use. Just as BIM has now become a tool that, under the duty of care, an architect may be expected to use on a project, AI-produced results will become part and parcel of the architect's professional judgement.

However, at least in today's AI systems, the complexity of the data structures that comprise neural networks are too great for humans to really understand, and those systems are trained with enormous data sets and measured by the validity of the outputs, not the specific computations that produced them. Kate Crawford, who writes on the challenges of AI implementation, describes this challenge well: 'In the case of AI, there is no singular black box to open, no secret to expose, but a multitude of interlaced systems of power. Complete transparency, then, is an impossible goal.'[9]

Opacity will make it impossible, in my view, for architects or others to rely on these systems without some sort of third-party validation of their results. Should the building industry, with architects as important contributors, decide to build a global data trust to drive AI, a component of that trust would include entities who would extensively test and certify the results of these systems before releasing them into the wild. The future leaders of BuildingSMART have a much bigger enterprise on their hands.

Beyond the proximate concerns of professional efficacy and certification, much work is currently underway to understand and evaluate the social and ethical dimensions of AI for decision-making. There are two important dimensions of this work. First, AI systems are trained from data that is the result of 'real world' inputs. Current natural language systems such as GPT-3 or facial recognition systems build their networks from scraping data, text or photographs from the internet, and as such that data has, inherently, the structural biases of its contributors. Princeton computer scientists who research this idea call it 'veridical' bias,[10] and suggest not only that is it is endemic in the world's data structures, but also a potential dashboard to understand social bias itself.[11]

A second dimension of AI only now beginning to be understood is its implications on the environment. In the now famous paper that resulted in her being fired from Google, computer scientist Timnit Gebru argues that the inherent environmental implications of building AI systems are underappreciated and accrue to the detriment of underprivileged communities who do not benefit from them. Calling natural language AIs like GPT-3, upon which Google increasingly relies, 'stochastic parrots', Gebru and her co-authors recommend that AI systems be designed to acknowledge the enormous contribution to atmospheric carbon they contribute by virtue of their intensive training, and rigorously curated to design out the inherent bias of available training data. Given that, for example, much of the content in the proposed data trust would likely be sourced from Western projects initially, carefully tending this data to be free of its obvious neo-liberal dynamics will be critically important.[12] Crawford further argues that the damage to the environment of extractive mining necessary to build the enormous compute infrastructure of AI is an externality that should be reflected in its cost and development.[13]

THE FUTURE OF DATA

With the advent of artificial intelligence systems, the building industry should be strongly motivated to share data beyond the solving of the near-term problem of the inefficiency that results from incompatible formats. Generating, consuming and properly curating digital design, construction and building operations data will allow these systems to be properly trained, and then unleash real power of computation for design. Doing so is an enormous opportunity for architects and their industry collaborators and comes with numerous pitfalls. However, perhaps the benefits of next generation technologies will finally motivate them to address and solve the larger questions of collaboration and integration, as well as ethical and environmental responsibility, that creating such a data source demands.

3.3 TASKS, AUTOMATED

>> AI WILL EXTEND THE RANGE OF AUTOMATED
PROCESSES AVAILABLE TO ARCHITECTS AND
CREATE OPPORTUNITIES FOR OTHER ASPECTS
OF OUR WORK TO BE FULLY AUTONOMOUS,
OPERATING IN PARALLEL WITH HUMAN
COUNTERPARTS. SUCH CHANGES ARE LIKELY
TO FIRST OCCUR IN THE TECHNICAL
OBLIGATIONS OF ARCHITECTS, AND MORE
SPECIFICALLY IN THE RELATIONSHIP BETWEEN
DESIGN AND CONSTRUCTION, WHERE AI-
ENABLED, AUTONOMOUS ANALYSIS CAN IMPROVE
THE EFFECTIVENESS AND CREDIBILITY OF
DESIGN AND PAVE THE WAY TO OTHER AI
CAPABILITIES. <<

3.3.1:
DOXEL'S
CONSTRUCTION
SITE INSPECTION
ROBOT, THEIR
FIRST ITERATION
OF SCANNING/
AI-BASED FIELD
VERIFICATION[1]

In 2018, BuildTech[2] start-up, Doxel, announced its first product, an AI-enabled robot that, rolling around like a tiny tank that can traverse rough terrain and even climb stairs, inspects a construction site using scanning and computer vision. It compares the results to BIM-based design information to determine construction progress on site. With the tagline 'Artificial Intelligence for Construction Productivity – Software that inspects quality and tracks progress so you can react in minutes, not months',[3] this system purports to evaluate the completeness, precision and installed value of work in place, automatically.

Meanwhile, in the analogue world of humans, standard services contracts for architects stipulate the architect's responsibility for construction administration (emphasis added):

>> *Carry out visual site inspections, as stated in item F of the Contract Details,* to review the general progress and quality of the works as they relate to the architectural design *and issue site inspection reports to the Client. (RIBA Standard Professional Services Contract 2020)[4]*

The Architect shall visit the site … to become generally familiar with progress and quality of the portion of the Work completed, and to determine, in general, if the Work observed is being performed in a manner indicating that the Work, when fully completed, will be in accordance with the Contract Documents. *However, the Architect shall not be required to make exhaustive or continuous on-site inspects to check the quality or quantity of the Work. (AIA B101-2017)[5]* <<

While here in America we clearly have a penchant for more turgid contractual definitions – a function of years of construction foibles and resulting litigation – the overlap is clear. Doxel's deep learning-enabled system is designed to either dramatically augment, or eliminate altogether, the need for human inspection of construction progress. It is a perfect example of the potential of AI in the design-to-construction process continuum: a Doxel robot uses computer vision and machine learning from other projects and related BIM, looking for something very specific ('is that column installed in the right place?'), and creates analytical results more quickly, cheaply and accurately than a person walking the construction site twice a day – an obligation specifically excluded from the AIA's definition of construction observation.

MISPLACED ANXIETIES

Doxel's value proposition – understanding and managing construction faster and more accurately – fits several trends that AI in building industry is likely to follow. Early investments in AI systems are:

» predominantly in the construction space (where there is more money spent, and to be had)

» focused on well-defined problems with technical inputs and outputs, and

» operates in the intersection of originating digital design data and construction execution (start with BIM, add computer vision, then measure progress).

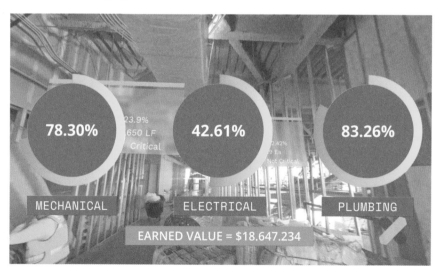

3.3.2:
DOXEL
ANALYSIS OF
CONSTRUCTION
COMPLETENESS[6]

The technical emphasis of this system, and many to follow, was anticipated early in the last technological transition to BIM by the architect Patrick MacLeamy, who created what is now known as the 'MacLeamy Curve', as seen in Figure 3.3.3.

Originally an argument for the efficacy of BIM for architects, MacLeamy posited that since the greatest value of the architect's work was early in the design process – where important decisions have the best chance of positively affecting results without disrupting progress – the bulk of our work process and value should shift to the earlier phases in the design-to-construction schedule. Further, he predicted that BIM would automate much of the production of technical documents and other information needed by contractors, making work in that portion of the scope of service far less valuable.

AI systems like Doxel's, which autonomously perform technical tasks that once required humans, is a logical extension of this same argument. However, while construction progress evaluation will clearly benefit from additional, digitally enabled help, a construction site is technically, geographically and, to some extent, politically complicated in a way that our little tank is unlikely to be able to fully understand. So our human architect, continuing to act on behalf of the client to protect her interests during construction, will continue to have

3.3.3:
THE MACLEAMY
CURVE

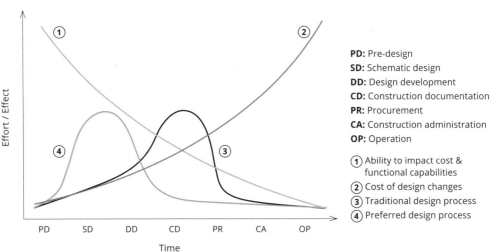

PD: Pre-design
SD: Schematic design
DD: Design development
CD: Construction documentation
PR: Procurement
CA: Construction administration
OP: Operation

(1) Ability to impact cost & functional capabilities
(2) Cost of design changes
(3) Traditional design process
(4) Preferred design process

a role even here (despite the likely reduction of human-required production tasks during the creation of working drawings, as argued in Chapter 1.5). In any case, since the technical aspects of design and construction – including document production and coordination, technical evaluation like code compliance or coordination, and managing and evaluating the information flow from the construction process – are the most likely candidates for AI-driven task automation, I remain convinced that anxiety by architects about being replaced as designers by autonomous AI is at best misplaced, and this argument was anticipated by MacLeamy in 2003.

RECONSIDERING RELATIONSHIPS

In Chapter 1.6, I defined the architect in terms of her relationships with four key constituents:

1.   As a protector of the public's health, safety and welfare.
2.   As an agent expert to the client.
3.   As a guide and translator of design intent to the builder.
4.   As a manager/leader/integrator to the balance of the design team.

Each of these roles requires the innate human ability to understand context, manage relationships and make trade-offs and judgements; these are tasks that are precisely the opposite capabilities of AIs, and particularly those whose neural networks require training in large, well-curated data sets. The multi-valent responsibilities of the architect, writ large as in this definition, are therefore unlikely to be replaced wholesale by computers, hence the argument, consistent with Susskind, about task replacement: limited tasks, perhaps, but complete supplanting by autonomous computerised agents, certainly not; and where tasks are AI-involved, they will be of a technical nature.

Of these four archetypal relationships which anchor the architect firmly in project delivery models, such technical task automation will alter most significantly the connection and obligations between the architect and the contractor/building supply chain. That relationship is the most transactional of the lot, characterised largely by exchanges of information, with the levels of precision and completeness often contested. AI systems will characterise, catalogue and eventually measure the quality of these interactions and connections in an effort to make those exchanges more effective. As the construction process is further automated by AI-assisted devices and systems, the demand for specific design information that is suited as input to those systems will increase, further tying architectural design to construction production in the name of efficiency. And as the demands for more intelligent supply chain decisions and management increase in an era of climate change, reduction of toxicity or even attempts to reduce forced labour, the architect's specification of materials will tie even more closely with an understanding of the supply itself. Contractors will therefore come to rely on architects for such intelligent decisions.[7] This is an inversion of the relationship of technology to design that emerged with the blob-makers of the 1990s, when the architect's digital shape-making tools made possible ever more elaborate forms that were left to engineers and builders to actualise.

The UK tendency to novate the architect's contract to the contractor after design, while simultaneously confusing and terrifying to this American architect, is consistent with the conclusion that design and construction can be operationally bound more tightly in contract, procedure and technology. As construction processes are more reliant on AI-based automation, the demand for logical relationships between design information and decision-making will naturally gravitate toward the design-construction interface.

PROCEDURAL PRODUCTION AND ITS POSSIBILITIES

So, an extension of this line of reasoning that includes MacLeamy's thesis, combined with the task analysis of the jobs of architects (see Figure 1.5.3 for the complete version, and Figure 3.3.4 for production work), suggests that the most likely opportunities for AI-based augmentation or automation of tasks is deep in the production phases of design, when a project is translated from design intent to the information readied for the contractor.

The automation of selected tasks of working drawing production is the best example to date of the implications of BIM in design. Working drawings today are more precise, better coordinated, more accurate and useful to contractors than their CAD predecessors, and BIM is a good platform, as both a representational schema and a training ground, for AI to continue this trend.

As many of the tasks of the working drawing phase are procedural in nature, it should be relatively straightforward to train AIs to perform them. Other objectives of the hand-off between designer and builder will still demand the judgement and coordination of the architect, who will be supported by machine intelligence in areas where large data sets, pattern matching and complex calculations and predictive algorithms could be of most use.

STANDARD SCOPES OF SERVICE

	3 SPATIAL COORDINATION	4 TECHNICAL DESIGN	NOT USED	5 MANUFACTURING + CONSTRUCTION	6 HANDOVER
RIBA (UK)					
AIA (US)	DD DESIGN DEVELOPMENT	CD CONSTRUCTION DOCUMENTS	PR PROCUREMENT	CA CONSTRUCTION CONTRACT ADMIN	NOT USED

SERVICE CATEGORIES

DEFINITION					
DESIGN					
PRODUCTION					
PROCUREMENT					
CONSTRUCTION					
OPERATION					

TASK COMPONENTS

DETERMINING CONFORMANCE TO THE BRIEF					
EVALUATING AND INTERGRATING TECHNICAL CONSIDERATIONS					
PERFORMING ENGINEERING ANALYSIS					
EVALUATING AND MANAGING PRODUCTION COSTS					
COORDINATING SPATIAL & TECHNICAL SYSTEMS					
COORDINATING SPATIAL & TECHNICAL SYSTEMS					
REVIEWING + APPROVING TECHNICAL DOCUMENTS					
REVIEWING CONSTRUCTION PROGRESS					

3.3.4: TASK ANALYSIS OF THE TECHNICAL/ PRODUCTION STAGES OF THE ARCHITECT'S WORK

PROCEDURAL

PROCEDURAL TO INTEGRATIVE

INTEGRATIVE

INTEGRATIVE TO PERCEPTIVE

To that end, consider the problem of construction cost projection, and particularly the heated negotiations oft held between designers and builders about conformance to target costs. The dimensions of this complex dance of data, judgement and computation are sketched in Figure 3.3.5.

Just as BIM was anticipated to accelerate aspects of cost estimating by automating the tasks of quantity take-off and calculation,[8] the various analytical tasks that converge to generate cost estimates, based on careful analysis combined with professional judgement, can generate greater insight and precision in cost projections – if AI were available in the following ways:

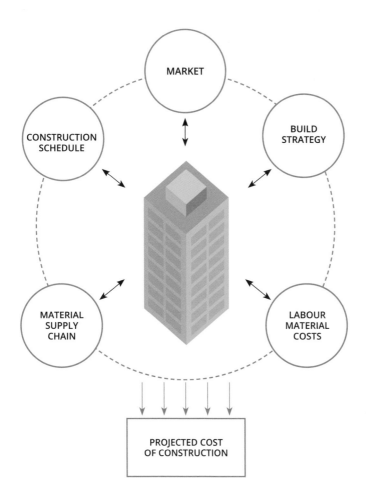

3.3.5:
ANALYTICAL
ELEMENTS OF
CONSTRUCTION
COST

Quantity surveying: Design documents define design intent, and builders must interpolate precise system characteristics, unspecified materials and implied construction elements in order to price them. By training on data sets that map construction documents to detailed previous take-offs, an AI could create these mappings from working drawings and create more accurate and historically informed bills of materials. The resulting data collections would be the basis of further training of the systems.

Market conditions: Macro-economic conditions introduce extreme volatility in construction pricing. Global or local circumstances change the availability of labour or the cost of materials more quickly than capital plans for projects can respond. This volatility is demonstrated by the difference between material purchase prices from manufacturers versus their cost as stockpiled in warehouses by builders in the US, as can be seen in Figure 3.3.6. At the time of writing, material prices have jumped as much as 40% (timber) since January 2021, as the US economy recovers from the pandemic; a similar pattern was seen in the recovery from the 2008 crisis. AI-based analysis and predictions, based on previous economic models and pricing profiles, could elucidate the potential implications for pricing, bidding and market conditions that affect cost models.

Cost of labour and materials: The costs of both labour and materials are estimated traditionally from historical information, but the actual pricing of projects generated by builders is a combination of historical data, in particular competitive advantages or disadvantages based on the builder's capabilities, as well as larger market forces such as the availability of skilled workers and other competitive pressures. A given builder or trade could train an AI from a combination of past projects to create a more reliable and accurate projection of such costs and map those projected costs to the designer's digital models to provide continuous cost modelling during the course of a project.

Supply chain conditions: The availability, price, performance and suitability of building materials is subject to many conditions in the delivery supply chain, from original sourcing to fabrication to delivery. Carbon implications of both embedded carbon and transportation costs, toxicity and labour equity (modern slavery) all affect the possibilities that a given material can be supplied to a project properly. AI systems could be trained on industrial material flow models, shipping manifests, bills of materials for sub-systems, even labour assessments, to factor these questions into cost projections of built assets.

Construction schedule: As most builders model the construction schedule for projects in order to plan and manage the build, such schedules could be training set for AI systems that would establish patterns and relationships between building typologies, construction locations, specific combinations of subcontractors and fabricators, and construction cost. The insights provided to builders could be provided, *a priori*, to design teams to understand whether a particular design was difficult or more expense to construct. Such information would be particularly useful in the concept stage, but it would allow a valid performance evaluation during technical production as well.

Build strategy: As contractors use increasingly sophisticated systems to model the sequence and methods of construction, these '5D' data sets instantiate libraries of construction logic at a macro-scale. With sufficiently large training sets they could be the basis for AI-generated construction planning. If the resulting projective modellers, which would become familiar with a wide variety of construction approaches and building types, could function as 'constructability evaluators' via AI-enabled simulators and were available to architects, the Albertian gap between intent and execution could be further closed.

The foregoing example, a speculation through the lens of a critical yet suboptimised dependency between design and construction, is meant to reinforce the idea that AI systems will appear first, and be most useful and efficacious, in the translation of design into technical performance, and particularly with regard to construction. Given the well-trod conclusion that the construction enterprise is unproductive and unpredictable, such improvements would be both welcome and embraced by architects, builders and their clients alike.[9]

CONSTRUCTING AUTOMATION

The painting robot we examined in Chapter 1.4 signals important changes for designers, not the least of which is the likelihood that their projects will be festooned with more precisely applied colours and textures. As Negroponte suggested in his early explorations of the automation of processes by machines, a first step towards incorporating digital technology is to use it to replicate an analogue process, and surely this is where our painting robot will begin. However, Negroponte further speculated that once these processes are fully integrated and understood, their capabilities will expand far beyond what their originators could have anticipated.[10] Our painting robot will improve its technique by repeatedly painting surfaces and sharing the lessons of its success and failures with other robots doing the same on other

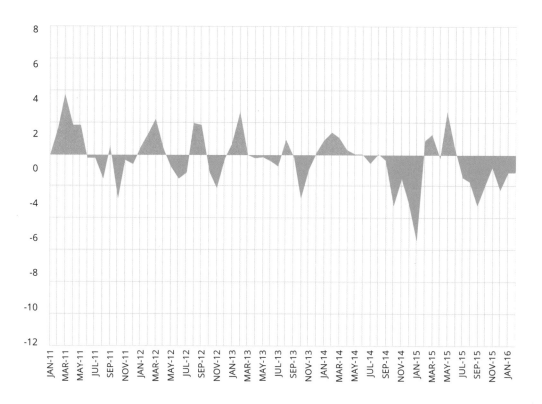

3.3.6:
MATERIAL
PRICE
VOLATILITY
IN THE US,
2006–21 [11]

projects. Further insights will be supplied by data coming from the construction supervision robots made by Doxel and their inevitable competitors. Eventually, the robotic painter will have AI-automated, autonomous colleagues installing and assembling other aspects of the construction project, and the procedures and protocols they generate could combine into an accessible, evolving source of construction insight that could truly modernise building.

For architects, this is a profound implication. It is not the automation of their tasks, so much as those of builders, that could close the divide between design intent and construction execution, a divide that Alberti defined six centuries ago and that has since characterised, or plagued, our industry. The instantiation of construction logic makes it available to the robots that enact it on site, but also to the designers who are configuring the eventual results of that robotic work. Where today an architect projects the eventual state of her design through a building information model, that design could be informed by a BIM connected to a construction simulator that might answer questions from as small as 'does that fit' to as large as 'can that be built?' In that sense, the task automation potential of AI enlarges, rather than diminishes, the potential of design.

3.3.7:
FOSTER +
PARTNERS
USING A BOSTON
DYNAMICS
ROBOT FOR
CONSTRUCTION
PROGRESS
ANALYSIS[11]

3.4 LABOUR OF DESIGN

>> THE LABOUR OF KNOWLEDGE WORKERS
LIKE ARCHITECTS, AS WITH MANY OF THEIR
PROFESSIONAL COUNTERPARTS, WILL LOOK
DIFFERENT WHEN MACHINES CAN PERFORM
ARCHITECTURAL TASKS. THE TYPES OF LABOUR
AND LABOURERS, THE STANDARDS UNDER
WHICH THEY OPERATE AND THEIR
INTERACTIONS WITH PRACTICES AND PROJECTS
WILL DEVELOP AS DIGITAL PLATFORMS
EVOLVE FROM INSTRUMENTS TO COGNITIVE
COLLABORATORS. <<

My first full-time job in an architect's office was in 1979, the pre-CAD era, when our work was taped to large drafting tables and prepared with plastic lead on giant sheets of mylar. The small office in Charlotte, North Carolina was known as a solid, if stolid, practice that did complete working drawings that resulted in routine buildings which did not leak or miss their budgets. I was assigned to help prepare construction documents for a bland shopping mall in Tennessee that still haunts my dreams.

There were about 20 or so of us in the drafting room – which I hesitate to call a studio, as there was so little design to speak of going on – at least two or three of whom were architectural draughtsmen (no women). These were older guys, some with architectural degrees, none with licenses, who drew and lettered beautifully, knew a lot of about how to put a building together, could never be in front of a client and were constant sources of knowledge to the younger, better educated but far less experienced architects-in-waiting like myself. In that era, many offices of any size had folk like this, whose main job was to draw, leaving all other architectural responsibilities to others. Late in my 15-month stint in this firm, the office manager began researching a new idea called 'computer-aided drafting', which the draughtsmen dismissed entirely as a gimmick.

TECHNOLOGY AND DESIGN LABOUR FROM DRAFTING TABLE TO BIM

Two decades later, these sorts of wise but unregistered drafters were largely missing from practices, unable to make the transition to CAD. Their jobs were replaced by young, digitally enabled CAD operators who were unafraid of the computer and had the skills to use it to draw. Almost no one in an architecture firm was trained or hired at this point as a drafter; young designers in training filled these roles. Just as today's secretaries no longer do much typing but are more general support staff, architectural jobs were no longer differentiated by

3.4.1:
THE DRAFTING
ROOM AT
SKIDMORE,
OWINGS &
MERRILL'S
OFFICE,
CHICAGO,
1958

production tasks (drafting) but more around roles and responsibilities (design, construction administration, specifications).

As firms are completely reliant on technology of all sorts these days, there are specialists in network management or even coordination of BIM data, but such roles are limited and certainly do not contribute to billable work. And even if yesterday's 'CAD monkeys' are today's 'BIM monkeys', BIM work is not routine drafting, as using a BIM tool requires a strong understanding of how a building goes together and how to properly represent it. But even today, while larger firms are hiring specialists in data management or, in some cases, software development, practice is largely devoid of technological specialists.

The advent of machine learning tools will reverse this trend. It will create demand for different sorts of architectural workers. As I have argued (see Chapter 2.4) that artificial general intelligence (AGI) is far in the future – particularly AGI that can step into the multi-faceted role of a proper architect – AI systems in architecture will be specific to tasks, technical in nature and will support the broader enterprise of design. Those systems will require specialised understanding of inputs, outputs, data demands and relationships of the AI system to the broader infrastructure of design information. These are skills that architects trained as generalists are unlikely to understand, nor, frankly, have much engagement with: the outputs of such systems will be of great interest; the process by which they are generated, not so much. While it would be nice to simply ask the 2030 version of Alexa, 'How much carbon is embodied in my project?' the route to that answer is likely significantly more complex.

TECHNOLOGY, SUPPLY AND DEMAND

I have argued up to this point that AI systems are likely to automate the more routine aspects of technical drawing production, data and document management, and information control. Just as today's 3D modelling platforms that generate high-resolution renderings have largely put professional (analogue and) digital renderers out of business, those jobs in offices will be lost.

However, there will be new jobs. Architecture will need experts who can manage these systems in production, particularly in relation to affiliated AI-based processes that will translate knowledge and insight from construction back to design. Complex technical analysis and building performance evaluation will be a necessary element of design generation. The dilemma for practices will be mapping demand for the specialists to handle such work and the available supply of talent. If an AI-based system is helping optimise the carbon footprint or forced-labour-free supply chain procurement of your building in the phase of conceptual design, that work is episodic at best, and probably punctuated with interactions with other intelligent systems. The data trust proposed in Chapter 3.2 will provide ubiquitous data, but using it well will be challenge.

In a recent survey of architectural and engineering professionals in Europe and the Middle East, 70% of firms reported that big data, data science and machine learning were important emerging technologies.[1] Far fewer are actually doing anything about it. Those firms trying to realise actual work from AI are competing – with limited success, I suspect – with the global demand for data scientists and machine learning experts, many of whom earn starting salaries well above those of their staff architects in UK practices.[2] While expertise in AI will grow in the next decade, matching supply and demand will be a challenge.

As Daniel Susskind argues in *A World Without Work: Technology, Automation and How We Should Respond* (the successor to *The Future of the Professions: How Technology Will Transform the Work Of Human Experts*), machine intelligence will, over time, take over responsibility for tasks rather than complete jobs. However, the aggregate task elimination in architecture will eliminate jobs, if for the simple reason that production-related activities such as creating working drawings or managing construction administration data comprise, at least in the USA, as much as 35% of a typical fee for an architect's services.[3] Automating this work, at least under current business models, means fewer workers. The so-called 'canonical model' described by Susskind – where jobs destroyed by innovation are replaced by the jobs required to create the new technologies – has given way to a new thesis, the so-called 'Autor-Levy-Murnane (ALM) Hypothesis', which declares that the routine tasks of work will be eliminated by computers, as those tasks are the easiest to teach machine learning systems to replicate. Skilled workers, like my early drafting colleagues, are eventually replaced, resulting in fewer jobs that do not reappear.[4]

Or at least fewer jobs will reappear than disappear, given the current demand for architects. However, there is another scenario, where AI technology empowers architects to the extent that demand for professionals – even those doing different jobs, like their counterparts in the early days of CAD – will be much higher. The history of BIM in the UK suggests that this might be the case, as demonstrated in Figure 3.4.2.

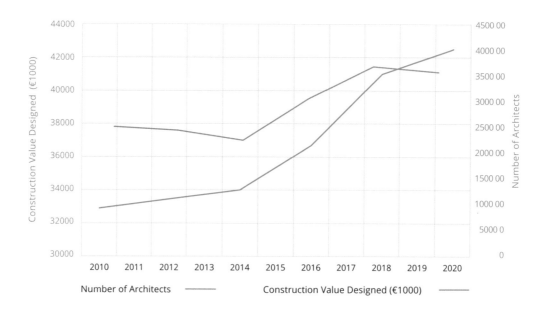

Number of Architects ——   Construction Value Designed (€1000) ——

3.4.2:
DEMAND FOR
UK ARCHITECTS
AND RELATED
CONSTRUCTION
VOLUME
DESIGNED[5]

Despite the inherent efficiencies introduced by BIM and its adoption driven by the Level 2 requirements, which in theory should have decreased architectural positions, and even despite a drop in designed construction value in 2020, the number of architectural positions in the UK has steadily increased for a decade. Perhaps better work begets more employment.

TALENT, SUPPLY AND DEMAND

Practice in the era of AI will therefore entail arbitraging the value of expert labour, machine production and data. The profession will need to find a way to access this talent across many scales of business, particularly since most firms, world-wide, are relatively small, averaging less than ten staff each.[6] While larger firms, with more human and financial resources, may get to AI capabilities first, for real change to be possible the wider profession must be able to access AI assets.

An intelligent design of the industry data trust described in Chapter 3.2 would entail a central marketplace for such talent and the infrastructure to make it accessible. The technologies of the so-called gig economy, which match demand with capacity, are the template for such a system. Like ride- and apartment-sharing services today, these systems use artificial intelligence themselves to align unused resources with those who might need them. Given that AI enactment in design practice will be task-oriented, perhaps the data trust might manage such a platform as part of the value proposition it puts forth to the global design industry.

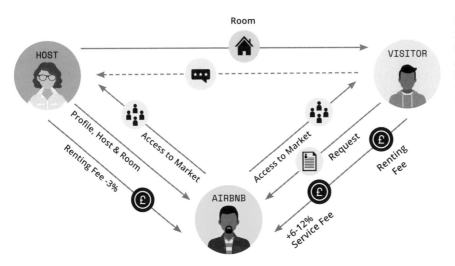

3.4.3:
BUSINESS
MODEL OF
AIRBNB,
MATCHING
HOUSING
CAPACITY WITH
TRAVELLER
DEMAND

More than a year of digitally enabled knowledge work by architects during the Covid-19 pandemic demonstrated that design work can be conducted with a relatively low loss of efficiency, with staff working remotely and distributed around the world. AI expertise could be similarly dispensed, making it more likely that this talent would be used fairly and effectively.

ETHICAL LABOUR AND AI

The architecture profession does not enjoy a sterling reputation for labour equity, and the advent of machine intelligence should not be seen as a strategy to extend that poor record. Salaries relative to other learned professionals are low,[7] steady jobs as uncertain as the economy and even the most well-known offices have well-earned reputations for labour abuse.[8] In the US, most architectural workers are exempt from labour laws that require employers to limit hours and provide minimum pay for overtime, characterising them as 'professional workers'. Doing rote CAD work, not so much; wrangling an AI, absolutely true.

Like any disruptive technology, AI offers opportunities and threats to the knowledge work of architects. As has been argued by my Yale colleague, Peggy Deamer, many architectural workers, particularly those who are unlicensed or less experienced, can be precarious workers whose work lives are destabilised by long hours, low pay, competitions and the generally poor management of human resources that many architects learn in the design studios of school (where time is considered an unlimited resource).[9] AI, like many of the automation technologies of the past, can be deployed in the interest of ruthless efficiency, with little consideration for the welfare of workers; ask anyone working today in an Amazon warehouse.[10] Systems that match workers with jobs have been demonstrated to instantiate the biases of the data set (like résumés of employed workers), denying qualified applicants opportunities generated by machine-based hiring systems. Workers in the extractive industries that drive modern computation are often exploited and unlikely to see any benefit from the computers they supply.

In her ill-fated paper for Google, Timnit Gebru makes the case that AI development must occur in parallel with an understanding of its broad implications. She suggests:

>> *Work on synthetic human behavior is a bright line in ethical AI development, where downstream effects need to be understood and modeled in order to block foreseeable harm to society and different social groups. Thus what is also needed is scholarship on the benefits, harms, and risks of mimicking humans and thoughtful design of target tasks grounded in use cases sufficiently concrete to allow collaborative design with affected communities.[11]* <<

Modelling downstream effects is what an AI-enabled future of design might look like. In architecture's case, the affected communities – including both our clients and our workers, and the profession – working in concert with providers and the academy, would best heed her advice and begin plotting the route to equitable AI today.

The ALM hypothesis (as discussed in Chapter 1.5) proposes that highly skilled workers – like the ones that will create, develop and manage AI – will remain in demand once machines carry out knowledge work. Very low-skilled but highly localised jobs, like those in personal services or dining, will also remain. In Susskind's 'massacre of the Dilberts', many jobs in between will be eliminated. Most architectural jobs in this scenario are probably safe, but the society for which we design buildings is likely to be dramatically affected. Like other issues of social equity, it is best to add this question to the list that the profession must address to responsibly design the built environment of the future.

3.5 VALUE PROPOSITIONS AND BUSINESS MODELS

>> TECHNOLOGICAL CHANGE IN ARCHITECTURE
HAS CHANGED THE PROCESSES, BUT NOT THE
VALUE, OF THE ARCHITECT'S SERVICES,
WHILE THE BUSINESS MODELS OF PRACTICE,
WHICH ORIGINATED CENTURIES AGO,
HAVE REMAINED STUBBORNLY IN PLACE.
AS THIS NEXT WAVE OF NEW TOOLS AND
CAPABILITIES WROUGHT BY INTELLIGENT
MACHINE AUTOMATION BECOMES APPARENT, THE
PROFESSION HAS ITS BEST CHANCE TO BREAK
THIS CYCLE BY REVISITING AND REVISING
ITS VALUE RELATIONSHIP TO THE BROADER
BUILDING INDUSTRY. <<

In his superb history of American architectural practice, *Assembling the Architect: The History and Theory of Professional Practice*, George Barnett Johnston explores the psyche of early 20th-century American architects through the eyes of one Tom Thumtack, the fictional alter ego of architect Frederick Squires, who wrote an illustrated volume about practice called *Architec-tonics: The Tales of Tom Thumtack, Architect*. Tom expounds on the anxieties of fees, as quoted by Johnson:

>> *We're paid on a percentage of the cost, but the capable architect is the one who keeps down the cost. Therefore, by doing his best he reduces his compensation... The client wants to keep the cost down, and his architect must help him in this, but the less the cost of a particular job, the less the compensation and the less likely to be the beauty of its execution from which the architect obtains his reputation.[1]* <<

Tom was explaining the seeming illogic of a system of compensation for architects that had, within it, two deep contradictions. First, when the architect's fee is based on a percentage of construction cost, the harder the architect works to bring the project into cost conformance, the less she is paid. Second, in the cases so common today when said fee is converted into a lump sum, the client has transferred the financial risk of the fee over to the architect, who perversely is now incentivised to work less, rather than more, to service that client, and thereby preserve some remainder of the fee as profit.

The idea that an architect should be paid in some proportion to the cost of construction seems to have originated centuries ago in Europe. Johnston explores this trajectory and quotes Benjamin Latrobe, the so-called 'first architect' of the United States, European-trained, British immigrant to America:

>> *It is in France, Germany & England the established custom of Architect (in England, confirmed by many decisions of the Courts) to charge for their works, 1., a commission of 5 prCent on the whole amount of the expence incurred in executing their design, -2., a certain sum for fair drawings, if furnished, according to their difficulty, number, or beauty; -3., if the work be at a distance from the usual residence of the Architect,-all traveling expences, & a certain sum pr day for loss of time.[2]* <<

The origins of today's percentage-of-construction-costs fees, adjusted by project complexity, plus reimbursable expenses of travel, are evident here and remain in place on both sides of the Atlantic today.[3]

COMMODITY RESISTANCE

It is hard to imagine another modern enterprise, even one so reluctant to really modernise like architecture, whose business models are essentially unchanged from their 18th-century precedents. Yet architecture, like much of the construction industry, remains tied to a fundamental value strategy of lowest first cost, where services are bid and purchased in a way not dissimilar to steel, sheetrock or carpeting: maximum pressure on competitive price, with far less attention paid to the value delivered, particularly over the cycle of a project's lifespan.

Neither of two immediate implications of AI for practice are particularly sanguine for architects, given our seemingly intractable business model. More productivity may provide short-term gains to the early adaptors, but such competitive advantages are short lived when eventually available to all competitors in the market and quickly fade.[4] Should AIs replace jobs in the architect's office, commoditised fees will fall in proportion, or worse.[5] Given this inevitable economic logic, finding new value propositions and business models will not just be nice benefits that accrue from these new technologies, but rather an existential necessity for the profession itself. If neither CAD nor BIM inspired such change, will AI?

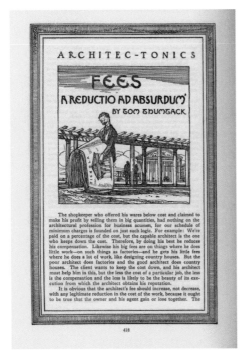

3.5.1:
KENT
ROCKWELL'S
'FEES: A
REDUCTIO
ABSURDUM' FROM
ARCHITECTURE
AND BUILDING,
46, 1914[6]

There is no question that those technologies improved the processes and, in some ways, the results of architectural services. CAD made drafting more accurate and efficient, while allowing architects to depict projects that were technically and formally more complex. BIM has allowed all members of the delivery team to generate, organise, integrate and exchange design information at much higher levels of resolution and transparency. It also, in some minimal way, begin to bridge the information gulf between design and construction; builders who saw the value of 3D data began to request it to assist their work. Other digital technologies have improved information exchange and client-facing images of projects (think renderings or even virtual reality models). Yet despite these improvements, the centuries-old methods for computing architectural computation remains largely intact, suggesting that these improved services have not translated into business terms, nor profit. The MacLeamy Curve, as described in Chapter 3.3, suggests that the real value of design work lies early in the delivery process, despite the relatively small degree of effort entailed there compared to production and delivery stages. Perhaps AI will begin the value shift.

A willingness to examine innovative business strategies for new services, organisational strategies and even new products can translate the threat of AI into an opportunity to improve both our performance as professionals and our business results, if we apply the same sort of creative thinking oft reserved for the design studio to this problem.

EXPLORING NEW VALUE

For the last several years we have offered a course at Yale called 'Exploring New Value Propositions of Design Practice', where our students are asked to interrogate the business models of architecture with the assumption that better jobs can be done designing them. Each semester, teams of students create what they believe to be the most provocative new models for practice, in response to the question: 'Where can the value of architectural services be best translated into a business model?' The projects are required to conform to just two conditions: the proposal must be based on something that a competent architect is capable of providing, and the compensation strategy must completely abandon any vestige of commoditised pricing, so no fixed or hourly fees allowed to make money.

By definition, this second constraint eliminates any option to extrapolate traditional practice, which is something of a pedagogical conceit intended to push the students far from the comfort zone with which they are familiar by dint of their professional experience and the businesses largely run by their professors. It does not imply, however, that there are no approaches for transfiguring traditional practice models towards new technologically inspired value, an idea we will examine later in this chapter.

After a few years of teaching this class, several consistent strategic themes emerged from the students' research, which range across the opportunities of services, organisation and products.[7] These ideas were congruent in that they could be mapped in relation to the connections between architects, clients and builders, as described graphically in Figure 3.5.2, and included:

- » *verticalisation strategies*, where the architect assumes her role plus at least one other traditional delivery role
- » *supporting strategies*, where the architect uses special skills, talents (and often technology) to provide a service to some part of the supply chain (including other architects)
- » *spanning strategies*, where a business derives value by creating an important connection between two sectors of the delivery model.

Should AI diminish the demand for architects, these approaches are a sketchy roadmap for other opportunities. However, they also suggest that the disruptive power of autonomous computing through intelligent machines might create new leverage and power for architects in the overall process of making buildings. For example:

A robust, AI-enabled design schema aimed at leveraging prefabrication and industrialised construction, based on procedural knowledge of manufacturing and assembly draws architects close enough to the means and methods of constructions so that they could perform sub-contracting or even construction management duties. There have been attempts to leverage BIM in similar ways as current precedent, tightly binding design strategy with construction, like SHoP Architects' early provision of digital fabrication data directly to the exterior enclosure fabricator in their Porter House project in New York.

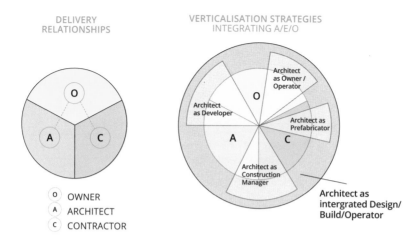

DELIVERY
RELATIONSHIPS

VERTICALISATION STRATEGIES
INTEGRATING A/E/O

Architect
as Owner /
Operator

Architect
as Developer

Architect as
Prefabricator

Architect as
Construction
Manager

Architect as
intergrated Design/
Build/Operator

O OWNER
A ARCHITECT
C CONTRACTOR

SUPPORTING STRATEGIES – SUPPORTING THE DELIVERY CHAIN

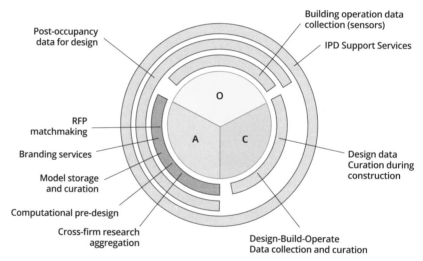

Post-occupancy
data for design

Building operation data
collection (sensors)

IPD Support Services

RFP
matchmaking

Branding services

Model storage
and curation

Computational pre-design

Cross-firm research
aggregation

Design data
Curation during
construction

Design-Build-Operate
Data collection and curation

3.5.2
DELIVERY
RELATIONSHIPS
AND
STRATEGIES OF
ALTERNATIVE
ARCHITECTURAL
PRACTICE
(FROM YALE
COURSE 2230B/
EXPLORING
NEW VALUE
PROPOSITIONS
OF DESIGN
PRACTICE) AND
A FEW EXAMPLE
BUSINESSES
SUGGESTED BY
THE STUDENTS
CLASSIFIED BY
THIS TYPOLOGY

SPANNING STRATEGIES – EXPANDING SCOPE

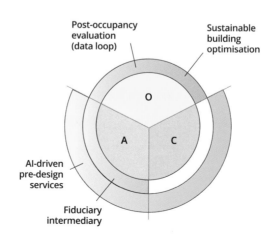

Post-occupancy
evaluation
(data loop)

Sustainable
building
optimisation

AI-driven
pre-design
services

Fiduciary
intermediary

A firm making a significant investment in an AI-based decision-making system that supports a specific technical design objective recoups the investment and makes a profit by offering the resulting expertise to other firms with similar challenges, or to clients as a validation service for other designs. An architect with deep expertise in a given discipline, say healthcare design, may have made a significant investment to develop AI-based analysis systems to evaluate or generate solutions in that building type. A healthcare practice, for example, might have transferred its deep knowledge of operating theatre layout into an AI that has been trained (with good and bad examples) from the global data trust. While their competitive advantage is in deploying the analytical results into the larger context of an overall solution for a hospital, the AI platform – which is very 'knowledgeable' about operating theatres – could be made available to other firms doing work (perhaps in another geographic location where competition is not an issue) or as a service to current hospital clients to evaluate their existing facilities. This could be a profitable business in and of itself, as well as a valid business development strategy to create new opportunities. As mentioned in Chapter 2.4, the current precedent today is Philadelphia architects Kieran Timberlake, who shares its expertise in energy assessment through its Tally© carbon assessment tool.

An architect with a long-term relationship with an institutional client – like a university or retail operator – has designed numerous buildings for them. Mapping design model data with data streams from building control operations systems,

3.5.3:
SHOP
ARCHITECTS,
PORTER HOUSE
ADDITION,
ELEVATION

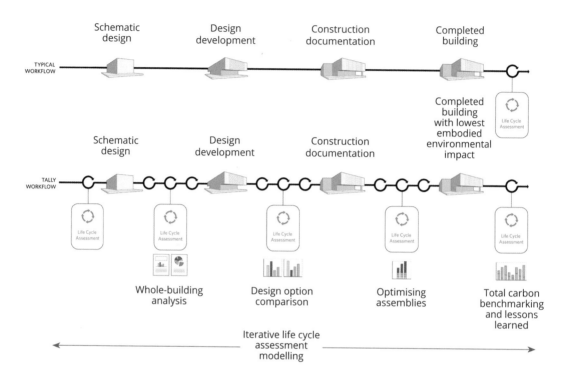

Schematic design   Design development   Construction documentation   Completed building

TYPICAL WORKFLOW

Completed building with lowest embodied environmental impact

Schematic design   Design development   Construction documentation

TALLY WORKFLOW

Life Cycle Assessment   Life Cycle Assessment   Life Cycle Assessment   Life Cycle Assessment   Life Cycle Assessment

Whole-building analysis   Design option comparison   Optimising assemblies   Total carbon benchmarking and lessons learned

Iterative life cycle assessment modelling

3.5.4:
TALLY®
CARBON
ASSESSMENT
TOOL

she has collected a large enough data base of this client's building base that, combined with data from the trust, has allowed the firm to create an AI-based optimisation tool that can apply to future designs as well as tuning the operation of current assets. The resulting contract, extending in blocks of five years post-occupancy for every building in the portfolio, requires the architect to manage and evaluate the data streams from projects, evaluate operational optimisation and make recommendations to the client. In addition to an annual service contract fee, the architect is also paid a small percentage of the operational savings in energy, maintenance and staffing resulting from these services. Today, architects EskewDumezRipple reserve 2% of fees to provide post-occupancy services to clients, discovering strategies for improving future projects and building credibility for new projects as well.[8]

TRANSFORMING BASIC SERVICES

These short vignettes are meant to stimulate thought about what alternative value propositions for architects, underpinned by the new capabilities of AI, might look like in the future. More important, however, are considerations of how, if at all, the basic services of architects at the core of our value – directly designing the built environment – may evolve when we share the job with intelligent machines. It is naïve to believe that architects can immunise themselves completely from the pressures of productivity improvements and knowledge work replacement that these systems will inevitably bring, and further that a profession that has operated with essentially the same business model since before the invention of electricity can, within a generation, turn to fundamentally new busines strategies. We are stuck with what we have, but can we fix it?

Facing these realities, which include continued competitive pressure to deliver our work as a commodity, there are two approaches that can reform, rather than completely replace, current fee-for-service approaches: reliability and results. Project uncertainty – the concern that project process will result in unexpected and unfortunate results – is a significant concern for architects, clients and builders alike.

A 2014 study in the United States quantified these worries, identifying the top causes for project instability as perceived by these constituents. While there is general agreement about the list of challenges, there is significant disagreement about their relative importance, as can be seen from the data in Figure 3.5.5.

3.5.5:
UNCERTAINTY
FACTORS IN
PROJECTS,
ACCORDING TO
A SURVEY OF
US DELIVERY
PARTICIPANTS[9]

OWNERS

ARCHITECTS

CONTRACTORS

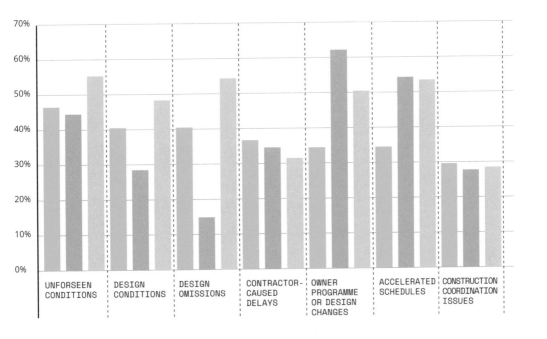

Of this list, two of the factors are the direct responsibility of the architect (design errors, omissions) and several more include the significant involvement of the architect in some way (owner changes, accelerated schedule and construction coordination). The resulting projects fail to perform, in some way, as seen in Figure 3.5.6.

The anxieties in Figure 3.5.5 portend failures of results in Figure 3.5.6.

Emerging AI strategies in construction give us a clue where this might be going. My former colleagues at Autodesk are developing a system that applies machine learning to construction administration data to identify potential problems on a job site – either in production or with specific contractors – in advance. A dashboard is shown in Figure 3.5.7.

Another provocative start-up, SmartVid.io, makes a tool that uses a combination of machine learning and computer vision to scan activity on a construction site and identify potential safety violations, as seen in Figure 3.5.8.

Note that neither of these companies is using AI to replace the work of human construction coordinators, risk managers or safety leaders, but rather augment their capabilities and allow them to significantly improve their performance. There is no reason why such an approach, applied to architectural design process, could not go right to the heart of client and contractor uncertainty in design process, be it checking for properly coordinated construction documents, cost prediction, lifecycle modelling of materials for durability/price trade-offs, and even missing information from the documents that comprise the contract for construction.

3.5.6:
WHEN
PROJECTS
MEET
EXPECTATIONS,
OR NOT[10]

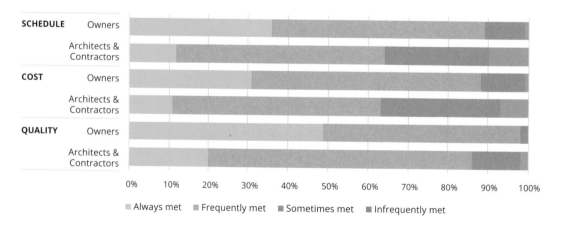

3.5.7:
PROBLEM
DASHBOARD
FROM BIM
360 IQ

Even generative design, where algorithms generate alternative design solutions, is not likely to be really useful until the resulting schemes can be sifted by intelligent evaluative systems driven by AI. Those systems can measure, mathematically, the performance of the resulting generated schemes, but choosing, refining and implementing those decisions will remain far beyond the reach of their capabilities, and human architects will always make the final determinations of what is best.

NUMERACY, CREDIBILITY VALUE

Z. Smith, the Director of Sustainability and Performance at EskewDumasRipple, believes that one key to success is for architects to reach what he calls 'numeracy': 'Illiteracy is about language, innumeracy is about numbers. We don't like numbers. It's not what people thought they were getting into when they went into architecture. But you have to do it if you want to make a good building.'[11] Architects largely measure the success of projects by an intangible sense of 'good' and 'bad' design, and size up the competition accordingly. As the respective chief technologists of three of the world's largest firms said to me once during an early BIM conversation: 'We don't compete with each other with technology. We beat each other on design.'

The definition of good design must move, at least in part, into the numerative, performance-based aspects of cost, quality and schedule – not to mention environmental and social impact – and the proper design and implementation of AI systems is the key to this change. Numerate and talented designers and the results they can create will have the dual benefits of increasing the credibility of architects and firmly anchoring our value in the building supply chain. And perhaps building an AI-assisted numeracy in setting performance objectives – and getting paid for them – will achieve the alignment of value and business models that Latrobe bemoaned almost three centuries ago.

CONCLUSION

>> THE PHILOSOPHER ARTHUR I. MILLER
DEFINES CREATIVITY AS 'THE PRODUCTION
OF NEW KNOWLEDGE FROM ALREADY EXISTING
KNOWLEDGE AND … ACCOMPLISHED BY PROBLEM
SOLVING'.[1] IN THAT SINGLE SENTENCE, HE
CAPTURES THE ESSENCE OF THE CHALLENGE FOR
ARCHITECTS AS ARTIFICIAL INTELLIGENCE
TECHNOLOGIES MATURE. <<

Our profession is, at its core, a creative enterprise that is valued for our ability to both define and solve problems in unique, appropriate and beautiful ways. Using AI should extend, rather than exterminate, that obligation to our clients and the public at large.

While it may take some time until it reaches the far corners of the design and construction professions, eventually the pattern analysis, autonomous processing and data evaluation capabilities of AI/ML will appear in the architectural landscape. We can declare, *a priori*, that the technology represents an existential threat to architects, or we can use our problem-solving skills and design a strategy that determines their ultimate destiny and use. And in doing so, we can increase the influence and credibility of architects with clients, mend decades of broken relationships with our construction collaborators and maybe even break the chain of our commoditised value propositions and stunted fee structures.

Any strategy for guiding the development and use of AI systems in architecture should serve two goals, to improve the quality of the built environment and to enhance the relevance of the human architects who are best suited to make those improvements through design. Given that the development of increasingly capable modes of automation are inevitable, I propose that the profession embrace five strategies to guide its future:

1. **Explicitly guide the definition and creation of technologies that will frame future practice.** Given that the next generation of technology may well define the future of architectural practice, the profession must establish means to declare its needs and direction in a way that does not defer to the business whims of software providers, whose motivations will ultimately prioritise profits and shareholders.[2] Architects have spoken with individual voices as customers rather than in a united fashion as a collective of important users. They should organise, collaborating with regulators, clients, designers and builders, to declare an industry technology strategy that prioritises the most important data and AI/ML capabilities and then demand the industry provide them. Contrary to common wisdom, software providers actually prefer such an approach, which saves them the time and effort of extensive and usually incomplete requirements research. The national BIM initiative in the UK, begun in 2010 and now a template for global technology adoption, is an excellent example of how this can be done at scale.[3]

2. **Expand the remit of design to include explicit performance.** Building performance is increasingly a necessary component of competent design. Starting with life safety at the beginning of the 20th century, and energy performance at the beginning of the 21st century, the range of performance parameters that architects must address will continue to expand. AI systems, driven by data, can empower architects to integrate a broader set of these parameters into their design processes, connecting the generation of solutions to performance models of, for example, occupancy, economics, epidemiological implications, embedded carbon and even embodied labour.[4] These considerations do not supplant the importance of design in its traditional sense, but rather expand it, while simultaneously enlarging the effectiveness of building and the credibility of architects.

3. **Create the data infrastructure that can serve as platforms for design.** Today's designers have created tens of thousands of digital models, mostly through BIM, of projects that represent an enormous resource for AI-generated insight. Contractors are doing the same with drone scans, computer-vision analysis of construction and digital construction management tools. Building control systems are generating huge lakes of digital information about systems performance. The potential of these resources is wholly unrealised without a strategy to organise and access them, particularly in the industry's contentious and risk-averse delivery models. The collaborative organisations described above could guide software strategy and create policy and platforms for the collection, organisation, access and use of this data, ostensibly through a global building data trust managed by a third-party fiduciary and accessible to all.

4. **Change the relationship between design, construction and asset operation.** The emergence of BIM as a broadly understood concept around 2004 coincided with the development of new models of integrated project delivery, based on the assumption that readily available, transparent sources of project information would accelerate cooperation between owners, designers and builders, the lack of which is a well-known pathology of the building industry.[5] More than 15 years later, that promise remains largely unfulfilled. Digital data created by the various players may be more transferrable, but it is often incompatible and rarely shared.[6] AI platforms, which could develop, manage and integrate the data relationships between these various representations and process, can be a catalyst for allowing architects to cross the traditional boundaries that separate project definition, design, construction and asset operation

and making knowledge reciprocally available across the design intent–construction execution divide. The tools may make the opportunity, but practitioners must want to embrace it.

5. **Shift the value propositions of design.** The commodification of the architect's services is a primary inhibitor of innovation and value creation by the profession.[7] Artificial intelligence tools strategically deployed in the service of performance-enhanced design solutions could be the catalyst for changing the fundamental business propositions of practice, converting the value of the architect's services from deliverables and fixed fees to outcome-based delivery models and related services. AI/ML systems could radically accelerate the capability of today's algorithmically driven software tools to predict the future state of project performance, generating best value by virtue of simulation. As soon as reliable AI-based tools – as a result of implementation of the previous four strategies – become widely available, architects could embrace the largest challenges of architecture and society, and finally escape the tyranny of commodified fees, limited resources and public scepticism about the value of the buildings they design.

The architect Eyal Weizman leads a London-based research team called Forensic Architecture, which is also the term that he uses to describe his 'investigative practice' that 'regards the common elements of our built environment – buildings, details, cities and landscapes, as well as their representations in media and as data – as entry points from which to interrogate contemporary processes and with which to make claims for the future'.[8] His team uses architectural approach methods supported by sophisticated data collection and analysis to examine political questions of government jurisdiction and use of force. The work is not traditional architecture in that it deconstructs information sources and reassembles them in ways that might not have been otherwise understood, using digital tools and analysis. Forensic Architecture's work – which is understandably highly controversial, especially to the governments he exposes – is a template for a strategy for AI in architecture as a whole. The data fragments that Forensic Architecture assembles for analysis are the basis for speculation about future states, which is a fundamental responsibility of an architect, especially those designing the built environment. To be able to make such claims about how design actions are manifest, as Weizman declares, architects need a critical stance about the collection, use and deployment of information about the world.

An obsessive reliance on data without such a critical view of its results could lead to disastrous results, particularly in a field of endeavour such as architectural design that purports to protect the public welfare. In early research on neural networks applied to medical treatments at a time when the internal logic of such systems was legible, ML platforms that yielded life-and-death decisions – even when such systems were generally reliable – led hospitals to wholly reject the use of AI. They became suspicious when the systems reported that asthma patients were less, rather than more, likely to suffer severe consequences from catching pneumonia, a clearly counter-intuitive result. Apparently, those patients are referred immediately to critical care early in the disease, and as such have far better outcomes. The neural network connected the inputs and the outputs, with no understanding whatsoever of what happened in between. Systems upon which such decisions are made must be both transparent and, in the case of professional judgement like architecture, validated externally.[9]

If the necessary data can be collected, and the systems validated, architecture can expand its remit dramatically. In a recent article addressing the fraught relationship between architecture and incarceration, Garrett Jacobs and Deanna Van Buren, leaders of the non-profit design alliance, Designing Justice + Designing Spaces, argue that architects must apply their skills to 'end the racism that is embedded in the built environment'. To create prototypes for their 'Alternatives to Incarceration Plan' for Los Angeles, they have implemented a design process deeply dependent on complex, interrelated data sources, explaining that 'We are partnering with data visualization, mapping and research organizations to understand how various systems – such as health care, first response, pre-arrest diversion, housing, post-incarceration re-entry, and more – interact at a district scale.'[10] In a pre-digital era, even collecting this data would have been impossible, much less evaluating it or deploying it as the basis for new design. At this juncture, when empiricist systems are coming to the fore, but cognition is largely missing, human designers play an irreplaceable role to direct data and marshal it. Only then will strategies for computation and design combined accomplish completely new results that humans create to improve our condition. This is the optimal outcome of the highest and best uses of artificial intelligence in architecture.

BIBLIOGRAPHY

Agrawal, A. Gans, J. and Goldfarb, A. *Prediction Machines: The Simple Economics of Artificial Intelligence*, Harvard Business Review Press, Boston, MA, 2018.

Alberti, L.B. *On the Art of Building in Ten Books*, MIT Press, Cambridge, MA, 1988. American Institute of Architects. 'AIA Document B101-2017: Standard Form of Agreement Between Owner and Architect', 2017, American Institute of Architects, Washington, DC: AIA, 2017.

– *The Architect's Handbook of Professional Practice: 15th Edition*. Wiley, Hoboken, NJ, 2014.

– *The Business of Architecture 2020*. American Institute of Architects. Washington, DC, 2020.

Anderson, S. 'Problem-Solving and Problem-Worrying', Lectures given at Architectural Association, London, March 1966 and ASCA Cranbrook, 5 June 1966.

Architects Council of Europe with Nacey Research. *The Architectural Profession in Europe 2020*, 2021.

Architects Registration Board. *ARB Criteria at Part 3 Prescription of Qualifications*. Architects Registration Board, 2012.

– *The Architects Code: Standards of Professional Conduct and Practice*, 2017.

Asadi, E. Li, B. and Chen, I. 'Pictobot: A Cooperative Painting Robot for Interior Finishing of Industrial Developments', *IEEE Robotics & Automation Magazine*, Vol. 25, issue June 2018, 2018, p 13.

Association of General Contractors of America. *Construction Inflation Report Q1 2021*, AGC America, Washington, DC, 2021.

Autor, D. 'Why are there Still So Many Jobs? The History and Future of Workplace Automation', *Journal of Economics Perspectives*, Vol. 29, issue 3, 2015, pp 3–30.

Baker, K. 'How Many Architects Does Our Economy Need?', *ARCHITECT*, 5 January 2018.

Baker, K. et. al. *Compensation Report 2019*, American Institute of Architects, Washington, DC, 2019.

Bernstein, H.M. *Managing Uncertainty and Expectations in Building Design and Construction*, McGraw Hill Construction Analytics, New York, 2014.

Bernstein, P. *Architecture, Design, Data: Practice Competency in the Era of Computation*, Birkhauser, Basel, 2018.

– 'Canonical Models of Architecture', *LOG: Model Behavior*, Vol. 50, issue 2021, pp 239–48.

Bernstein, P. and Deamer, Peggy. *BIM In Education*, Yale University School of Architecture, NH, 2011.

Bernstein, P. 'Intention to Artifact' in *Digital Workflows in Architecture: Design–Assembly–Industry*, ed. Scott Marble, Birkhäuser, Basel, 2012.

– 'The Distractions of Disruptions: Technical Supply in an Era of Social Demand', *Architectural Design (AD)*, Vol. 90, issue 2, 2020, pp 11.

– 'Innovative Tools in the Movement Toward Slave-Free Building', in Sharon Price, Harriet Harriss, Phillip Bernstein, Susan Jones, Christ Sharples and Michael Green (eds), Grace Farms/Pratt Institute Seminar Series, 2020.

BIM Industry Working Group. *BIM Management for Value, Cost & Carbon Improvement: A Report for The Government Construction Client Group*, UK Government Department of Business, Innovation and Skills.London, https://www.hse.gov.uk/construction/areyou/principal-designer.htm, 2021 (accessed 6 June 2021).

Brockman, J. *Possible Minds: Twenty-five Ways of Looking at AI*, Penguin Press, New York, 2019.

Brynjolfsson, E. and McAfee, A. *The Second Machine Age: Work, Progress, and Prosperity in a Time of Brilliant Technologies*, W.W. Norton & Company, New York, 2014.

Brynjolfsson, E. and T. Mitchell. 'What Can Machine Learning Do? Workforce Implications', *Science*, Vol. 358w, https://doi.org/10.1126/science.aap8062, 2017 (accessed 27 December 2020).

Brynjolfsson, E. and A. McAfee. 'Will Humans Go the Way of Horses? Labor in the Second Machine Age', *Foreign Affairs*, Vol. 94, issue 4, 2015, pp 8-14.

Carpo, M. *The Alphabet and the Algorithm*, MIT Press, Cambridge, MA, 2011.

– *The Digital Turn in Architecture 1992–2012,* Wiley, Chichester, 2013.

– *The Second Digital Turn: Design beyond Intelligence*, MIT Press, Cambridge, MA, 2017.

Carr, N.G, 'IT Doesn't Matter', *Harvard Business Review*, https://hbr.org/2003/05/it-doesnt-matter, 2003 (accessed 15 June 2021).

Christian, B. *The Alignment Problem: Machine Learning and Human Values*, W.W. Norton & Company, New York, NY, 2020.

Corcoran, H. 'Architecture Schools Adapt to an Uncertain Future', *Architectural Record*, May 2020, 2020, p 1.

Crawford, K. *Atlas of AI: Power, Politics, and the Planetary Costs of Artificial Intelligence*, Yale University Press, NH, 2021.

Davis, D. 'Architects Versus Autodesk', *Architect Magazine*, 27 August 2020.

Deamer, P. and Bernstein, P. *Building (in)the Future: Recasting Labor in Architecture*, Princeton Architectural Press. New York, 2009.
Deamer, P. *The Architect as Worker: Immaterial Labor, The Creative Class, and the Politics of Design*, Bloomsbury Academic, London and New York, 2015.

Deltek Clarity with Longitude. *Deltek Clarity Architecture and Engineering Industry Study: Trends and Benchmarks in EMEA and APAC*, Deltek, 2021.

Dickson, B. *DeepMind scientists: Reinforcement Learning is Enough for General AI. BDTechTalks.com*. https://bdtechtalks.com/2021/06/07/deepmind-artificial-intelligence-reward-maximization/, 2021 (accessed 9 June 2021).

– *Why AI Can't Solve Unknown Problems. BDTechTalks.com*, https://bdtechtalks.com/2021/03/29/ai-algorithms-representations-herbert-roitblat/, 2021 (accessed 8 June 2021).

Domingos, P. *The Master Algorithm: How The Quest For The Ultimate Learning Machine Will Remake Our World*, Basic Books, a member of the Perseus Books Group, New York, 2015.

BIBLIOGRAPHY

Egan, J. *Rethinking Construction: The Report of the Construction Task Force* http://constructingexcellence.org.uk/wp-content/uploads/2014/10/rethinking_construction_report.pdf, 1998 (accessed 10 April 2021).

Folkens, B. 'Chihuahua or Muffin?', *Cloudsight*, https://blog.cloudsight.ai/chihuahua-or-muffin-1bdf02ec1680, 2017 (accessed 29 December 2020).

Ford, J. and Galliford, T. *Information Management According to BS EN ISO 19650–Guidance Part C: Facilitating the Common Data Environment (Workflow and Technical Solutions)*, UK BIM Alliance, London, 2020.

Gallaher, M. et. al. *Cost Analysis of Inadequate Interoperability in the U.S. Capital Facilities Industry*, US Department of Commerce Technology Administration, 2004.

Gebru, T., Bender, E., McMillan-Major, A. and Mitchell, M. 'On the Dangers of Stochastic Parrots: Can Language Models Be Too Big?' *FaccT'21*, Virtual, Canada, 2021.

Grace Farms Foundation. *Design for Freedom*, Grace Farms Foundation, 2021.

Gutman, R., Cuff, D., Wriedt, J. and Bell, B. *Architecture from the Outside In: Selected Essays*, Princeton Architectural Press, New York, 2010.

Hao, K. *The Coming War on the Hidden Algorithms that Trap People in Poverty*, MIT Technology Review, https://www.technologyreview.com/2020/12/04/1013068/algorithms-create-a-poverty-trap-lawyers-fight-back/, 2020 (accessed 1 April 2021).

– *These Weird, Unsettling Photos Show That AI Is Getting Smarter*, MIT Technology Review, https://www.technology-review.com/2020/09/25/1008921/ai-allen-institute-gen-erates-images-from-captions/, 25 September 2020 (accessed 4 March 2021).

– *Inside The Fight to Reclaim AI from Big Tech's Control*, MIT Technology Review, https://www.technologyreview.com/2021/06/14/1026148/ai-big-tech-timnit-gebru-paper-ethics/, 14 June 2021 (accessed 20 March 2021).

Heaven, W. *AI Is Learning How To Create Itself*, MIT Technology Review, https://www.technologyreview.com/2021/05/27/1025453/artificial-intelligence-learning-create-itself-agi/, 27 May 2021 (accessed 6 June 2021).

Higgin, G., Jessop, W.N. and the Tavistock Institute of Human Relations London, *Communications In The Building Industry: The Report of a Pilot Study*, Tavistock Publications, London, 1965.

Hosey, L. 'Going Beyond the Punchlist: Why Architects Should Embrace Post-Occupancy Evaluations', *Metropolis*, https://www.metropolismag.com/architecture/architecture-post-occupancy-evaluations/, 2019 (accessed 15 June 2021).

Illich, I. *Disabling Professions*, M. Boyars, London and Salem, NH, 1977.

McKinsey Company. *An Executive's Guide to AI*, https://www.mckinsey.com/business-functions/mckinsey-analytics/our-insights/an-executives-guide-to-ai, 2020 (accessed 12 December 2020).

– *The Next Normal in Construction: How Disruption is Reshaping the World's Largest Ecosystem*, 2020.

– *Reinventing Construction: A Route to Higher Productivity* https://www.mckinsey.com/industries/capital-projects-and-infrastructure/our-insights/reinventing-construction-through-a-productivity-revolution, 2017 (accessed 16 June 2021).

Jacobs, G. and Van Buren, Deanna. *Decarceration and Designing to Divest*. Architectural Record, https://www.architecturalrecord.com/articles/14828-commentary-decarceration-and-designing-to-divest, 5 October 2020 (accessed 6 October 2020).

Jha, S. *Can You Sue an Algorithm for Malpractice? It Depends*, STAT, https://www.statnews.com/2020/03/09/can-you-sue-artificial-intelligence-algorithm-for-malpractice/, 2020 (accessed 25 October 2021).

Johnston, G.B. *Assembling The Architect: The History and Theory of Professional Practice*, Bloomsbury Visual Arts, London, 2020.

Leach, N. 'Design in The Age of Artificial Intelligence', *Landscape Architectural Frontiers*, Vol. 6, issue 2, 2018, pp 8-19.

– 'Do Robots Dream of Digital Buildings?' in *1st International Conference on Computational Design and Robotic Fabrication (CDRF 2019)*, ed. Philip F. Yuan et al. , Springer, Beijing, China, 2020.

Marcus, G. and Davis, E. *Rebooting AI: Building Artificial Intelligence We Can Trust*, Pantheon Books, New York, 2019.

Marcus, G. *The Next Decade in AI: Four Steps Towards Robust Artificial Intelligence*. Unpublished manuscript, *https://arxiv.org/abs/2002.06177*, 2020 (accessed 20 December 2020).

– 'Artificial Intelligence Is Stuck. Here's How To Move It Forward', *The New York Times*, 30 July 2017.

McNulty, N. *Introduction to Bloom's Revised Taxonomy*, https://www.niallmcnulty.com/2019/12/introduction-to-blooms-taxonomy/, 2019 (accessed 7 March 2021).

Metz, C. *One Genius' Lonely Crusade to Teach a Computer Common Sense*, Wired, https://www.wired.com/2016/03/doug-lenat-artificial-intelligence-common-sense-engine/, 24 March 2016 (accessed 27 December 2020).

Miller, A.I. *The Artist in The Machine: The World f AI Powered Creativity*, The MIT Press, Cambridge, MA, 2019.

Mokyr, J., Vickers, C. and Ziebarth, N.L. 'The History of Technological Anxiety and the Future of Economic Growth: Is This Time Different?', *Journal of Economic Perspectives*, Vol. 29, issue 3, 2015, pp 31-50.

Moretti, E. and ProQuest. *The New Geography of Jobs*, Houghton Mifflin Harcourt, Boston, 2012.

Mumford, S. and Anjum, R. *Counterfactuals and Causal Inference: Methods and Principles for Social Research* (Analytical Methods for Social Research), Oxford University Press, New York, 2014.

NBS. *10th Annual BIM Report 2020*, NBS, London, 2020.

National Council of Architectural Registration Boards. *Architect Registration Examination® (ARE®) 5.0 Handbook*, NCARB, Washington. DC, 2020.

Negroponte, N.*The Architecture Machine*, MIT Press, Cambridge, MA, 1970.

Parman, J. 'Is Architectural Licensing Necessary?' *Common Edge*, https://commonedge.org/is-architectural-licensing-necessary/, 2020 (accessed 31 October 2020).

Pearl, J. and Mackenzie, D. *The Book of Why: The New Science of Cause and Effect*, Basic Books, New York, 2018.

Pelli, C. *Observations for Young Architects*, Monacelli Press, New York, 1999.

Peña, W. and Parshall, S. *Problem Seeking: An Architectural Programming Primer*, Wiley, New York, 2001.

Picon, A. *What About Humans? Artificial Intelligence in Architecture* in *1st International Conference on Computational Design and Robotic Fabrication (CDRF 2019)*, ed. Philip F. Yuan et al., Springer, Beijing, China, 2020.

Rabenek, A. *The Place of Architecture in the New Economy*, Routledge, Abingdon, Oxon, 2016.

Rittel, H. and Webber, M. *Dilemmas in a General Theory of Planning*, *Policy Sciences*, Vol. 4, issue 2, 1973, pp 155-69.

Rowe, P. 'A Priori Knowledge and Heuristic Reasoning In Architectural Design', *Journal of Architectural Education*, Vol. 36, issue 1, 1982, pp 18-23.

Royal Institute of British Architects. *RIBA Plan of Work 2020 Overview*, RIBA, London, 2020.

– 'Standard Professional Services Contract 2020: Architectural Services', RIBA, London, 2020, p. 48.

Ruhaak, A. 'How Data Trusts Can Protect Privacy', *MIT Technology Review*, https://www.technologyreview.com/2021/02/24/1017801/data-trust-cybersecurity-big-tech-privacy/, 2021 (accessed 3 May 2021).

Russell, S.J. *Human Compatible: Artificial Intelligence and the Problem of Control*, Viking, New York, 2019.

Scheer, D. *The Death of Drawing: Architecture in the Age of Simulation*, Routledge, London and New York, 2014.

Schön, D.A. *The Reflective Practitioner: How Professionals Think in Action*, Basic Books, New York, 1983.

Simonite, T. 'What Really Happened When Google Ousted Timnit Gebru', *Wired*, https://www.wired.com/story/google-timnit-gebru-ai-what-really-happened/, 2021 (accessed 10 June 2021).

Slavid, R. 'RIBA Contracts CPD Day Review', *Architecture.com*, https://www.architecture.com/knowledge-and-resources/knowledge-landing-page/riba-contracts-cpd-day-review, 2019 (accessed 6 June 2021).

Spiro, A., Ganzoni, D. and Carpo, M. *The Working Drawing: The Architect's Tool*, Park Books, Zurich, 2013.

Squires, F. and Kent, R. *Architec-tonics: The Tales of Tom Thumtack, Architect*, The William T. Comstock Company, New York, 1914.

Staff, T. 'A Wave of Venture Capital Is Pouring Into Construction Tech Sector', *The Real Deal: Real Estate News*, https://therealdeal.com/national/2019/07/03/a-wave-of-venture-capital-is-pouring-into-construction-tech-sector/, 2019 (accessed 29 December 2020).

Steenson, M. *Architectural Intelligence: How Designers and Architects Created the Digital Landscape*, The MIT Press, Cambridge, MA, 2017.

Susskind, D. *A World Without Work: Technology, Automation, And How We Should Respond*, Metropolitan Books/Henry Holt & Company, New York, 2020.

Susskind, R. and Susskind, D. *The Future of the Professions: How Technology Will Transform the Work of Human Experts*, Oxford University Press, Oxford, 2015.

The Infrastructure and Projects Authority, *Government Construction Strategy 2016–20*, Cabinet Office, London, 2016.

Thurairajah, N. and Goucher, D. *Advantages and Challenges of Using BIM: a Cost Consultant's Perspective* in *49th Annual Associates Schools of Construction Conference*, ed. California Polytechnical State University, San Luis Obispo, California, 2013.

Till, J. *Architecture Depends*, MIT Press, Cambridge, MA, 2009.

Tombesi, P. *On the Cultural Separation of Design Labor Building (In) the Future: Recasting Labor in Architecture*, eds P. Deamer and P. Bernstein, Princeton Architectural Press, New York, 2010.

Turing, A. 'Computing Machinery and Intelligence', *Mind*, Vol. 59, issue 236, October 1950, pp 433-60.

UK Building Information Alliance. *Information Management According to BS EN ISO 19650 – Guidance Part 1: Concepts*. buiildingSMART, London, 2019. UK Health and Safety Executive. *Are You a Principal Designer?* https://www.hse.gov.uk/construction/areyou/principal-designer.htm, 2016 (accessed 6 June 2021).

– *Principal Designers: Roles and Responsibilities*, https://www.hse.gov.uk/construction/cdm/2015/principal-designers.htm, 2015 (accessed 7 June 2021).

Wakabayashi, D. *Meet the People Who Train the Robots (to Do Their Own Jobs)*, https://www.nytimes.com/2017/04/28/technology/meet-the-people-who-train-the-robots-to-do-their-own-jobs.html, 2017 (accessed 11 April 2020).

Weizman, E. *Forensic Architecture: Violence at the Threshold of Detectability*, Zone Books-The MIT Press, Brooklyn, NY and Cambridge, MA, 2017.

Witt, A. *Shadow Plays: Models, Drawings, Cognitions*, LOG: *Model Behavior*, Vol. 50, issue 2021, pp 29-38.

Yuan, P.F. Xie, M., Leach, N., Yao, J. and Wang, X, *Architectural Intelligence Selected Papers from the 1st International Conference on Computational Design and Robotic Fabrication (CDRF 2019)*, https://yale.idm.oclc.org/login?URL=https://doi.org/10.1007/978-981-15-6568-7, 2019 (accessed 1 May 2020).

Yudkowsky, N. and Bostrum, N. *The Ethics of Artificial Intelligence*, Cambridge Handbook of Artificial Intelligence, Cambridge University Press, Cambridge, 2011.

Zarkadakis, G. '"Data Trusts" Could Be the Key to Better AI', *Harvard Business Review*, https://hbr.org/2020/11/data-trusts-could-be-the-key-to-better-ai, 2020 (accessed 11 June 2021).

Zweig Group. *2019 Fee & Billing Survey*. Zweig Group Consulting, Fayetteville, AR, 2019.

REFERENCES

INTRODUCTION

1 For reference, the MacBook Pro laptop I am writing on at this moment has 16GB of internal memory, or 62,500 times more as that ill-fated PDP-11. It also has yet to catch fire.

2 https://en.wikipedia.org/wiki/PDP-11 (accessed 5 July 2021).

3 David R. Scheer, *The Death of Drawing: Architecture in the Age of Simulation*, Routledge, London and New York, 2014.

4 Richard E. Susskind and Daniel Susskind, *The Future of the Professions: How Technology Will Transform the Work of Human Experts*, Oxford University Press, Oxford, 1st edn, 2015, xiv, p 1.

5 This particular text was created by a system called InferKit, which you can try yourself at https://appinferkit.com/generate (first accessed 21 April 2021).

6 Personal email exchange with Dr Mark Greaves of Pacific Northåwest National Laboratory, 27 November 2020.

7 Erik Brynjolfsson and Andrew Mcafee, *The Second Machine Age: Work, Progress, and Prosperity in a Time of Brilliant Technologies*, W.W. Norton & Company, New York, 1st edn, 2014.

8 Neal Leach has done interesting work on this question, including the article about computation, design and dreaming: Neil Leach, 'Design in the Age of Artificial Intelligence', *Landsc. Archit. Front.*, 6/2, 2018, pp 8–19.

9 Peter G. Rowe, 'A Priori Knowledge and Heuristic Reasoning in Architectural Design', *Journal of Architectural Education*, 36/1, 1982, pp 18–23.

10 Daniel Susskind, *A World Without Work: Technology, Automation and How We Should Respond*, Metropolitan Books/Henry Holt & Company, New York, 1st edn, 2020.

1.1

1 Among the varied histories of technology in architecture, those by Mario Carpo are perhaps the most prescient, particularly Mario Carpo, *The Alphabet and the Algorithm*, 'Writing Architecture', MIT Press, Cambridge, MA, 2011, xi, and Mario Carpo, *The Second Digital Turn: Design Beyond Intelligence*, 'Writing Architecture', MIT Press, Cambridge, MA, 2017.

2 See © RMN-Grand Palais / Art Resource, NY.

3 This argument is made in detail in Carpo, *The Alphabet and the Algorithm*.

4 Architecte au plan, <https://cdli.ox.ac.uk/wiki/doku.php?id=architecte_au_plan> (accessed 11 April 2021).

5 Leon Battista Alberti, *On the Art of Building in Ten Books*, MIT Press, Cambridge, MA, 1988, xxiii.

6 Annette Spiro, David Ganzoni and Mario Carpo, *The Working Drawing: The Architect's Tool*, Park Books, Zurich, 2013, p 279.

7 See Nicholas Negroponte, *The Architecture Machine*, MIT Press, Cambridge, MA, 1970.

8 One distinct advantage of paper-based information exchange is that it requires no special software nor data standards, beyond graphic convention, to transmit or translate it between originator and consumer.

9 The aerospace, automotive and manufacturing design disciplines had deployed modelling tools decades before architects. Similarly, the form-making and rendering tools of movies and games (such as Autodesk's Maya) were appropriated by architects once they ran on sufficiently affordable machines.

10 See hypar.io (accessed 11 April 2021).

11 For example, see McKinsey & Company, 'An executive's guide to AI', <https://www.mckinsey.com/business-functions/mckinsey-analytics/our-insights/an-executives-guide-to-ai?cid=other-eml-alt-mip-mck&hdpid=d36c6b61-313b-431c-b3d4-141bc805e7e2&hctky=11625380&hlkid=36ab108977a849a2ba50687fd2e467de>, 2020 (accessed 20 November 2020).

12 Steve O'Hear, 'Spacemaker, AI software for urban development, is acquired by Autodesk for $240M', <https://techcrunch.com/2020/11/17/spacemaker-ai-software-for-urban-development-is-acquired-by-autodesk-for-240m/>, 2020 (accessed 24 November 2020).

13 Phillip G. Bernstein, *Architecture, Design, Data: Practice Competency in the Era of Computation*, Birkhäuser, Basel, 2018, p 23.

14 Ajay Agrawal, Joshua Gans and Avi Goldfarb, *Prediction Machines: The Simple Economics of Artificial Intelligence*, Harvard Business Review Press, Boston, MA, 2018.

15 Spiro et al., *op. cit.*, p 280.

1.2

1 This quote from Walter Gropius can be found in a superb history and analysis of Nicholas Negroponte's early work on architectural technology: Molly Wright Steenson, *Architectural Intelligence: How Designers and Architects Created the Digital Landscape*, MIT Press, Cambridge, MA, 2017, p 18.

2 Ibid., p 170.

3 Noam Chomsky at MIT, Terry Winograd at Stanford University and Roger Schank at Yale University (with whom I studied in the late 1970s) each put forth competing theories of cognition from which various early AI efforts developed.

4 Gary Marcus and Ernest Davis, *Rebooting AI: Building Artificial Intelligence We Can Trust*, Pantheon Books, New York, 2019, p 41.

5 See 'AI Winter', <https://en.wikipedia.org/wiki/AI_winter> (accessed 29 December 2020).

6 This technology is known as 'neural networks' and operates, in part, on a form of statistical correlation called Bayesian probability.

7 Joseph Paul Cohen, Paul Bertin and Vincent Frappier, 'Chester: A Web Delivered Locally Computed Chest X-Ray Disease Prediction System', *ArXiv*, abs/1901.11210 (2019).

8 See 'Alphago Zero Cheat Sheet', <https://medium.com/applied-data-science/alphago-zero-explained-in-one-diagram-365f5abf67e0> (accessed 11 April 2021).

9 A frequently cited example of AI is the teaching of ML systems to recognise pictures of cats. Rather than directly program the computer to understand what a cat looks like, the systems were trained to study millions of pictures of cats (readily available on the internet). Eventually, the

computer could learn to recognise an image of a cat. This process, through various technological improvements, has been extended to other large data sets, like all the text ever posted online. It is not always successful, however; see Brad Folkens, 'Chihuahua or Muffin', *Cloudsight*, 2017, <https://blog.cloudsight.ai/chihuahua-or-muffin-1bdf02ec1680>

10 See Pedro Domingos, *The Master Algorithm: How the Quest for the Ultimate Learning Machine Will Remake Our World*, Basic Books, New York, 2015.

11 Gary Marcus, 'The Next Decade in AI: Four Steps Towards Robust Artificial Intelligence', 2020, p 51, <https://arxiv.org/ftp/arxiv/papers/2002/2002.06177.pdf> (accessed 19 December 2020).

12 For an explanation of a theory of computational causality (and a compelling argument against a statistical view of knowledge), see Judea Pearl and Dana Mackenzie, *The Book of Why: The New Science of Cause and Effect*, Basic Books, New York, 2018.

13 This is a convention I always use, in my writing and in the classroom, as a way of acknowledging that the expectation is traditionally 'his'.

14 See 'Cyc', <https://en.wikipedia.org/wiki/Cyc> (accessed 31 December 2020).

15 See Stanford Anderson, 'Problem-Solving and Problem-Worrying', Lectures given at the Architectural Association, London, March 1966 and ASCA Cranbrook, 5 June 1966, as referenced by Steenson, *Architectural Intelligence: How Designers and Architects Created the Digital Landscape*. An intermediate step between problem-solving and problem-worrying, as Anderson defined it, might be William Peña's strategy for problem-seeking, an approach to defining an architectural problem before diving headfirst into the design process itself. His definitive text on the topic, originally written in 1977, was updated in 2001; see William Peña and Steven Parshall, *Problem Seeking: An Architectural Programming Primer*, Wiley, New York, 2001.

16 Peter G. Rowe, 'A Priori Knowledge and Heuristic Reasoning in Architectural Design', *Journal of Architectural Education*, 36, no. 1, 1982.

17 There are several examples of the early uses of empiricist systems, primarily in construction. Software maker Autodesk has applied ML techniques to construction administration data to anticipate process failures (such as delays or change orders); BuildTech start-up Smartvid.io uses computer vision and ML to discover job site safety concerns. See <www.smartvid.io> (accessed 30 December 2020).

18 Cade Metz, 'One Genius' Lonely Crusade to Teach a Computer Common Sense', *Wired*, 24 March 2016.

19 Marcus, *op. cit.*, p 3.

20 Ibid., p 27.

21 Personal conversation with Mark Greaves, 18 December 2020.

22 See Niall McNulty, 'Introduction to Bloom's Revised Taxonomy', <https://www.niallmcnulty.com/2019/12/introduction-to-blooms-taxonomy/> (accessed 15 December 2020).

23 After the now infamous Move 37 when AlphaGo defeated world Go champion Lee Sedol, Demis Hassabis, the CEO of Google's AI research project DeepMind, said: 'It doesn't play like a human and it doesn't play like a program. It plays in a third, almost alien way.' Cade Metz, 'In Two Moves, AlphaGo and Lee Sedol Redefined the Future', *WIRED* (2016). <https://www.wired.com/2016/03/two-moves-alphago-lee-sedol-redefined-future/> (accessed 11 July 2021).

24 This model mirrors one created by McKinsey Consulting that used to explain the possibility of AI in a business context, where the classifications are 'Descriptive/Predictive/Prescriptive'. See McKinsey & Company, 'An Executive's Guide to AI', <https://www.mckinsey.com/business-functions/mckinsey-analytics/our-insights/an-executives-guide-to-ai> (accessed 18 December 2020).

25 Pedro Domingos, *op. cit*, p xxi.

26 Marcus, *op. cit.*, p 3.

1.3

1 Richard E. Susskind and Daniel Susskind, *The Future of the Professions: How Technology Will Transform the Work of Human Experts*, Oxford University Press, Oxford, 2015, p 22.

2 See Ivan Illich, *Disabling Professions*, Ideas in Progress, M. Boyars, London and Salem, NH, 1977.

3 Donald A. Schön, *The Reflective Practitioner: How Professionals Think in Action*, Basic Books, New York, 1983, p 5.

4 Horst W.J. Rittel and Melvin M. Webber, 'Dilemmas in a General Theory of Planning', *Policy Sciences* 4, no. 2, 1973.

5 For statistics on the generally dismal state of architectural graduates, see Kermit Baker et al., 'Compensation Report 2019', American Institute of Architects, Washington, DC, 2019).

6 Of note for this particular comparison is the exchange programme that has existed between Yale and the University of Cambridge for many years, where one graduate from each programme receives a full scholarship to attend the other school. Despite the professionally certified credentials granted by each, the graduates from each reciprocal program cannot use their degree to qualify for licensure in the opposite country.

7 See 'Master of Architecture I Professional Degree Program', <https://www.architecture.yale.edu/academics/programs/1-m-arch-i> (accessed 8 January 2021) for a detailed list of course requirement for the M.Arch 1 degree, which qualifies a successful graduate to sit for the ARE.

8 National Council of Architectural Registrations Boards (NCARB), 'Architect Registration Examination® (Are®) 5.0 Handbook', Washington, DC: NCARB, 2020.

9 Architects Registration Board (ARB), 'ARB Criteria at Part 3 Prescription of Qualifications', ed. Architects Registration Board, 2012.

10 For an eloquent exploration of some of these differences in opinion, see Jeremy Till, *Architecture Depends*, MIT Press, Cambridge, MA, 2009.

REFERENCES

11 Stuart J. Russell, *Human Compatible: Artificial Intelligence and the Problem of Control*, Viking, 2019, p 87.

12 Ibid., p 20.

13 See Mario Carpo, *The Second Digital Turn: Design Beyond Intelligence*, 'Writing Architecture', MIT Press, Cambridge, MA, 2017.

14 These images can be generated at the Allen Institute for AI, <https://vision-explorer.allenai.org/text_to_image_generation> (accessed 8 January 2021), as described in Karen Hao, 'These weird, unsettling photos show that AI is getting smarter', *MIT Technology Review*, 25 September 2020.

15 A favourite example is www.thiscatdoesnotexist.com (accessed 8 January 2021), an AI-driven site that creates photorealistic images of cats that it conjures based on vast collections of pictures of cat faces, a resource infinitely available on the internet. The site creates very realistic feline visages but could not answer even a basic question about its subjects.

16 See Phillip G. Bernstein, *Architecture, Design, Data: Practice Competency in the Era of Computation*, Birkhäuser, Basel, 2018.

17 César Pelli, for whom I worked during this time, was particularly adept at this, and seemed to have an encyclopaedic memory for materials, plan configurations, and other knowledge of past projects at the ready during any design review. While looking at the proposed plan for, say, a new office tower, he would ask everyone: 'Remember the second version of the core that we suggested for the first tower at Canary Wharf? That would work here.' Those of us who were younger, and far less experienced, found this ability both extremely useful and incredibly daunting.

1.4

1 As it was 1979, every single architect on the floor, save one, was a white male.

2 For a superb history and analysis of Negroponte's early work on architectural technology, see Molly Wright Steenson, *Architectural Intelligence: How Designers and Architects Created the Digital Landscape*, MIT Press, Cambridge, MA, 2017.

3 As quoted by Daniel Susskind in Daniel Susskind, *A World Without Work: Technology, Automation and How We Should Respond*, Metropolitan Books/Henry Holt & Company, New York, 2020, p 129.

4 Neil Leach, 'Do Robots Dream of Digital Buildings?', paper presented at the 1st International Conference on Computational Design and Robotic Fabrication (CDRF 2019), Beijing, China, 2020.

5 Antoine Picon, 'What About Humans? Artificial Intelligence in Architecture', Architectural Intelligence: Selected Papers from the 1st International Conference on Computational Design and Robotic Fabrication (CDRF 2019), ed. Philip F. Yuan et al., p 22.

6 Susskind, *op. cit.*, p 43.

7 Richard E. Susskind and Daniel Susskind, *The Future of the Professions: How Technology Will Transform the Work of Human Experts*, Oxford University Press, Oxford, 2015, p 271.

8 Andrew Witt, 'Shadow Plays: Models, Drawings, Cognitions', *LOG: Model Behavior*, 50, 2021.

9 The International Standards Organization (ISO) has developed data and process workflow standards for building projects based on Building Information Modelling (BIM) technologies and data. The standard requires creation of a Common Data Environment, which is defined at https://www.iso.org/obp/ui/#iso:std:iso:19650:-1:ed-1:v1:en, Section 3.3.15 (accessed 1 February 2021).

10 This robot is designed to paint an interior wall in concert with a human painter, see B. Li, I. Chen and E. Asadi 'Pictobot: A Cooperative Painting Robot for Interior Finishing of Industrial Developments', *IEEE Robotics & Automation Magazine*, 25 June 2018, p 85.

1.5

1 Richard E. Susskind and Daniel Susskind, *The Future of the Professions: How Technology Will Transform the Work of Human Experts*, Oxford University Press, Oxford, 2015, p 1.

2 Ibid., p 94.

3 While the theoretical construct of parametric, 3D modelling had been around for decades before the term 'Building Information Modelling' and viable tools for its use became available on or about 2002, very widespread adoption did not occur until almost 20 years later. The American Institute of Architects reported in its 2020 Firm Survey that approximately 80% of US firms were BIM capable in 2019, an extremely slow adoption curve for any new technology.

4 Daniel Susskind, *A World Without Work: Technology, Automation and How We Should Respond*, Metropolitan Books/Henry Holt & Company, New York, 2020, pp 38–39.

5 Ibid., p 73.

6 Niall McNulty, 'Introduction to Bloom's Revised Taxonomy', <https://www.niallmcnulty.com/2019/12/introduction-to-blooms-taxonomy/> (accessed 7 March 2021).

7 Susskind, *op. cit.*, p 78.

8 Stuart J. Russell, *Human Compatible: Artificial Intelligence and the Problem of Control*, Viking, New York, 2019, p 87.

9 Royal Institute of British Architects (RIBA), 'RIBA Plan of Work 2020 Overview', RIBA, London, 2020.

10 American Institute of Architects, 'B101-2017 Standard Form of Agreement between Owner and Architect', American Institute of Architects, Washington, DC, 2017.

11 Russell, *op. cit.*, p 86.

1.6

1 Typical models vary by the role of the contractor, the relationship between the designer and the builder, the number of contracts between various participants and the client, and the timing of ascertaining the cost of construction. Examples include 'design-bid-build', 'public-private partnership', and 'integrated project delivery'. For a detailed explanation of such models in the United States, see American Institute of Architects, *The Architect's Handbook of Professional Practice: 15th Edition*, Wiley, Hoboken, NJ, 2014, Chapter 9.1 'Project Delivery Methods', p 508.

2 Sir John Egan is generally credited with formulating the basis of this concern and laying the groundwork for modern uses of technology and alternative project delivery models, at least in the UK. See Sir Roger Egan, 'Rethinking Construction: The Report of the Construction Task Force' (1998). However, the systematic exploration of these questions may be seen to have begun much earlier by the National Joint Consultative Committee of Architects, Quantity Surveyors and Builders in a study prepared by the Tavistock Institute of Human Relations; see Gurth Higgin, William Neil Jessop and the Tavistock Institute of Human Relations London, *Communications in the Building Industry; the Report of a Pilot Study*, Tavistock Publications, London, 2nd edn, 1965.

3 Even when designers and builders use digital tools, the exchange of digital information – mostly drawings – is still limited by traditional concerns about precision and liability, resulting in enormous inefficiencies as information is recreated along each step in the delivery process: design, fabrication, and construction. That inefficiency is leading to modern attempts to integrate and streamline the process. For example, the list of companies that prefabricate large portions of buildings lengthens each fiscal quarter: Bryden Wood, Blockable, DIRTT, FabCab, and Mace, to name a few. The author is a collaborator on a study of such companies to be published in 2022.

4 Higgin, Jessop and the Tavistock Institute of Human Relations London, *op. cit.*, p 77.

5 See 'Design Intent' in the Designing Buildings Wiki at <https://www.designingbuildings.co.uk/wiki/Design_intent> (accessed 11 April 2021).

6 Higgin, Jessop and Tavistock Institute of Human Relations London, *op. cit.*, p 40.

7 For an excellent exploration of this evolution in the United States, see George Barnett Johnston, *Assembling the Architect: The History and Theory of Professional Practice*, Bloomsbury Visual Arts, London, 2020.

8 Another variation of delivery models current in vogue is called

'Design Assist', where certain aspects of the project, typically the mechanical and electrical systems, are designed by the engineer of record, but final traditional working drawings are omitted and the design itself is documented in detail in shop drawings prepared by the subcontractor who is going to fabricate and install the system. This approach acknowledges that the actual, useful value of 'design intent' construction documents for such systems is minimal, and therefore they can be abandoned.

9 Higgin, Jessop and Tavistock Institute of Human Relations London, *op. cit.*, p 43.

10 See McKinsey & Company, 'The Next Normal in Construction: How Disruption Is Reshaping the World's Largest Ecosystem', 2020.

11 Paolo Tombesi, 'On the Cultural Separation of Design Labor', *Building (in) the Future: Recasting Labor in Architecture*, eds. Peggy Deamer and Phillip G. Bernstein, Princeton Architectural Press, New York, 2010.

12 Andrew Rabeneck, 'The Place of Architecture in the New Economy', *Industries of Architecture*, eds. Katie Lloyd Thomas et al, Routledge, Abingdon, Oxon, 2016, p 192.

13 Ibid., p 192.

2.1

1 See 'Creative Destruction', <https://en.wikipedia.org/wiki/Creative_destruction> (accessed 30 April 2021).

2 Daniel Susskind, *A World Without Work: Technology, Automation and How We Should Respond*, Metropolitan Books/Henry Holt & Company, New York, 2020, p 35.

3 At this writing in mid-2021, there are several such companies offering early planning analysis studies created by AI-driven generative design processes, including Autodesk's Spacemaker AI, Sidewalk Lab's Delve, and start-ups Envelope and Plot-Z.

4 In the US-based office where I was practising in 1990, a single PC-based computer with monitor and software exceeded $25,000 per workstation, more than $50,000 escalated to 2021. That cost is almost equal to the annual salary of the young architect who operated it.

5 Revenue numbers from AIA Firm Surveys of 2006 and 2014, overlaid with employment data from Kermit Baker, 'How Many Architects Does Our Economy Need?' in *ARCHITECT*, 2018, 5 January 2018.

6 Economic data on the performance of the US architectural industry is exceedingly difficult to collect, as the best potential source, the AIA, is constrained, as described below, from collecting and evaluating it. As such, this chart was derived from a combination of AIA sources, specifically the work of Kermit Baker cited in n. 5, plus additional information provided by the AIA by email in May 2021, along with profitability data generated by the Zweig Group consulting company, which does not have the same legal nervousness as AIA. Zweig, however, tracks both architects and engineers, so the profit data is likely more volatile than if only architects were considered. Finally, the AIA collects firm data on a very irregular basis, so intervening years (indicated by the hatch marks on the graph) are extrapolated from available data on revenue (indicated by the solid blue bars). Sources: personal correspondence with Kermit Baker, 15 May 2021; AIA Firm Surveys 'The Business of Architecture', 2002, 2005, 2008, 2011, 2013, 2015, 2017, 2019; Zweig Group, '2019 Fee & Billing Survey' in *Fee & Billing Surveys*, Zweig Group Consulting, Fayetteville, AR, ed. Will Swearingen, 2019, p 208.

7 I have been engaged in an ongoing conversation with the Chief Economist of the American Institute of Architects, Kermit Baker, about this question. I have no doubt that Kermit could easily generate a metric for productivity in the American profession, where he is the primary researcher responsible for decades of bi-annual *Business of Architecture* surveys. However, owing to two anti-trust sanctions enforced by the US Justice Department on the AIA, Kermit must stay far from issues of compensation, relative levels of effort and their relationship. This likely makes creating any productivity measurement system nearly impossible, and thus these surveys are silent on this topic.

REFERENCES

8 The origins of this argument can be found, in the pre-AI era, in Phillip G. Bernstein, 'Intention to Artifact', in *Digital Workflows in Architecture: Design–Assembly–Industry*, ed. Scott Marble, Birkhäuser, Basel, 2012.

9 For a provocative exploration of data that enables AI and its ethical and economic implications in the era of big tech, see Kate Crawford, *Atlas of AI: Power, Politics, and the Planetary Costs of Artificial Intelligence*, Yale University Press, New Haven, CT, 2021.

10 Private conversation between Mark Greaves of the Pacific Northwest National Laboratory and the author, 16 April 2021.

11 See Anouk Ruhaak, 'How Data Trusts Can Protect Privacy' in *MIT Technology Review*, 24 February 2021.

2.2

1 Karen Hao, 'The Coming War on the Hidden Algorithms That Trap People in Poverty' in *MIT Technology Review*, 2020, <https://www.technologyreview.com/2020/12/04/1013068/algorithms-create-a-poverty-trap-lawyers-fight-back/> (accessed 6 June 2021).

2 Royal Institute of British Architects, 'Standard Professional Services Contract 2020: Architectural Services', RIBA, London, 2020, p 48.

3 American Institute of Architects, 'Document B101 - 2017: Standard Form of Agreement between Owner and Architect', American Institute of Architects, Washington, DC, 2017.

4 Health and Safety Executive of HM Government, 'Are you a principal designer?', <https://www.hse.gov.uk/construction/areyou/principal-designer.htm> (accessed 6 June 2021).

5 National Council of Architectural Registration Boards, 'Legislative Guidelines and Model Law – Model Regulations 2016–2017', NCARB, Washington, DC, 2016.

6 According to both RIBA and AIA sources, a vast majority of architects in both countries are using BIM tools today. See NBS, '10th Annual Bim Report 2020', NBS, London, 2020, p 9, and American Institute of Architects, 'The Business of Architecture 2020', American Institute of Architects, Washington, DC, 2020, p 30.

7 UK Architects Registration Board, 'The Architects Code: Standards of Professional Conduct and Practice', 2017, p 14.

8 National Council of Architectural Registration Boards, *op. cit.*, p 6.

9 Remember that you do not actually own that software, you are merely licensing its use for your purposes, and those purposes had best conform to the extensive terms and conditions of the EULA, which you are very unlikely to have bothered to read.

10 See 'Autodesk LICENSE AND SERVICES AGREEMENT', <https://download.autodesk.com/us/FY17/Suites/LSA/en-us/lsa.html> (accessed 6 June 2021).

11 During my time at Autodesk, the roadmap for a typical annual release of Revit was in thirds: one each for design, coding and testing.

12 Recent assertions by AI-enabled technology giants such as Facebook and Twitter reinforce this prediction, as each has asserted that they are mere 'platforms' with little or no responsibility for the consequences of their use by customers. See, for example, 'Zuckerberg says Facebook not responsible for US Capitol Riots' at <https://www.ft.com/content/39a699fc-1730-4a5d-b43e-634ebe189d79> (accessed 6 June 2021).

13 According to news reports, 'with the "sole exception" of the Royal Borough of Kensington and Chelsea – which accepted that the refurbishment work should not have been signed off – all organisations had denied responsibility in "carefully crafted statements"'. See 'Grenfell Tower fire: Inquiry told firms "deny responsibility"' at <https://www.bbc.com/news/uk-51256738> (accessed 6 June 2021).

14 John J. Parman, 'Is Architectural Licensing Necessary?' in *Common Edge*, 2020, <https://commonedge.org/is-architectural-licensing-necessary/> (accessed 6 June 2021).

15 See Daniel Susskind, *A World Without Work: Technology, Automation and How We Should Respond*, Metropolitan Books/Henry Holt & Company, New York, 2020.

2.3

1 Or, in a limited number of US states, by a licensed structural engineer.

2 Health and Safety Executive (HSE), 'Principal designers: roles and responsibilities', 2015, <https://www.hse.gov.uk/construction/cdm/2015/principal-designers.htm> (accessed 7 June 2021).

3 For a detailed explanation of American phases of work, see American Institute of Architects, *The Architect's Handbook of Professional Practice: 15th Edition*, Wiley, Hoboken, NJ, 2014.

4 It is instructive that there is no British counterpart to the American phase of 'Procurement', when contractors compete to be selected for construction of the project. This implies that design and construction activities in the US are possibly more separated, and early contractor involvement less likely. In contrast, the lack of clear definition of the architect's role in translating the design into a price in the UK system suggests little responsibility by designers and far more control, earlier in design, by UK builders.

5 Leon Battista Alberti, *On the Art of Building in Ten Books*, MIT Press, Cambridge, MA, 1988.

6 This interpretation of Alberti has been put forward by the historian Mario Carpo, specifically in Mario Carpo, *The Alphabet and the Algorithm*, 'Writing Architecture', MIT Press, Cambridge, MA, 2011.

7 See Antoin Picon's 'What About Humans? Artificial Intelligence in Architecture' in Philip F. Yuan et al., *Architectural Intelligence, Selected Papers from the 1st International Conference on Computational Design and Robotic Fabrication* (Cdrf 2019), <https://yale.idm.oclc.org/login?URL=https://doi.org/10.1007/978-981-15-6568-7> (accessed 6 June 2021).

8 See Judea Pearl and Dana Mackenzie, *The Book of Why: The New Science of Cause and Effect*, Basic Books, New York, 2018.

9 See Judea Pearl, 'The Limitations of Opaque Learning Machines' in John Brockman, *Possible Minds: Twenty-Five*

Ways of Looking at AI, Penguin Press, New York, 2019, p 17.

10 Ibid., p 23.

11 Daniel C. Dennett, 'What Can We Do' in Brockman, p 52.

12 Ibid., p 51.

13 See Grace Farms Foundation, 'Design for Freedom', Grace Farms Foundation, 2021. <https://www. designforfreedom.org/wp-content/ uploads/2020/10/DesignforFreedom_ FullReport_L.pdf> (accessed 7 June 2021).

14 Dennett in Brockman, p 46.

2.4

1 As quoted in Ben Dickson, 'Why AI can't solve unknown problems', *BDTechTalks.com* (2021), <https:// bdtechtalks.com/2021/03/29/ai- algorithms-representations-herbert- roitblat/> (accessed 8 June 2021).

2 For two examples of early but unrequited enthusiasm for BIM, see Phillip Bernstein and Peggy Deamer, eds., *BIM in Education*, Yale University School of Architecture, New Haven, CT,: 2011; Phillip G. Bernstein and Peggy Deamer, eds. *Building (in) the Future: Recasting Labor in Architecture*, Princeton Architectural Press, New York, 2009.

3 It is an oversimplification to attribute this failure to the academy alone. The building industry adopts new technologies and processes at a glacial pace, and curricula evolve even more slowly, even when there may be advocates for exploiting the opportunities of new tools on the faculty (which is also rare). Software vendors (like my former employer) share some of the responsibility here as well, having failed to support academic engagement with BIM while simultaneously dramatically slowing the maturation and development of BIM platforms as they become more profitable to sell. See https://letters- to-autodesk.com/letter-to-autodesk. pdf, 'An open letter that reflects customer perspectives on Autodesk 2020' (accessed 11 June 2021).

4 See Liverpool's Building Information Modelling and Digital Transformation (BIM-DT) MSc or the University of North Carolina/Charlotte's Dual Master of Science in Architecture / Master of Science in Computer Science or Information Technology.

5 Of the 120 credit hours necessary to achieve the equivalent 'Part 2' professional degree in Yale's Master of Architecture/First Professional Degree, nine are attributed to courses in visualisation, where theoretical or historical material is connected to drawing or digital tools. One summer course of three credits is dedicated directly to BIM, in connection with a building construction and documentation requirement.

6 Dennett in John Brockman, *Possible Minds: Twenty-Five Ways of Looking at AI*, Penguin Press, New York, 2019, p 46.

7 Russell in ibid., p 32.

8 NCARB, '2012 Ncarb Practice Analysis of Architecture', (National Council of Architectural Registration Boards, 2013). Note that at the time of this writing, NCARB was completing the 2020 Practice Analysis.

9 The technical definition can be found as the UK BIM Standard and ISO 19650; see <https://www. ukbimframework.org/standards- guidance/> (accessed 8 June 2021).

10 UK, The Infrastructure and Projects Authority, 'Government Construction Strategy 2016–20', Cabinet Office, London, 2016.

11 UK BIM Alliance, 'Information Management According to Bs En Iso 19650 – Guidance Part 1: Concepts', buildingSMART, London, 2019.

3.1

1 Leon Battista Alberti, *On the Art of Building in Ten Books*, MIT Press, Cambridge, MA, 1988.

2 Mario Carpo, *The Alphabet and the Algorithm*, 'Writing Architecture', MIT Press, Cambridge, MA, 2011, p 167.

3 Ibid., p 21.

4 This pursuit of design perfection, which is of course not possible (nor legally advisable as a warranty of completeness) is the source of much unfortunate behaviour first learned in school and then transported to the office studio.

5 This is the characterisation of such systems by computer scientist Mark Greaves. Personal correspondence between the author and Greaves, 7 June 2021.

6 Those systems use the current technique called reinforcement learning, where the system is programmed to try alternative strategies and instantiate successes and reject failures; they are the current rage among AI programmers in 2021, as described in Ben Dickson, 'DeepMind Scientists: Reinforcement Learning Is Enough for General AI', *BDTechTalks.com*, 2021, <https:// bdtechtalks.com/2021/06/07/ deepmind-artificial-intelligence- reward-maximization/> (accessed 8 June 2021).

7 This is not to say that certain, highly constrained building types that operate on strict templates and are relatively simple to create – e.g. a fast-food restaurant or an Apple Store – might not be suitable for AI generation. But most projects are so site- and condition-specific that it is difficult to imagine an AI sophisticated enough to manage competing design constraints and trade-offs.

8 See Chapter 2.1, 'The Digital Transformation of Design' in Phillip G. Bernstein, *Architecture, Design, Data: Practice Competency in the Era of Computation*, Birkhäuser, Basel, 2018.

9 Cost modelling in the early stages of a project are parametric (area × cost/unit of area), where later in a project estimates are based on quantitative take-offs (measurements of installation × cost of materials and labour). It will be important for any such system to differentiate these approaches based on the resolution of the design.

10 Carpo, *op. cit.*, p 21.

11 These accusations are typically in the form of architects 'not knowing how a building goes together,' or 'how one would really build that'.

12 Ajay Agrawal, Joshua Gans and Avi Goldfarb, *Prediction Machines: The Simple Economics of Artificial Intelligence*, Harvard Business Review Press, Boston, MA, 2018, p 24.

REFERENCES

3.2

1 See 'BuildingSMART', <https://en.wikipedia.org/wiki/BuildingSMART> (accessed 11 June 2021).

2 During my time at Autodesk, I served in various capacities with BuildingSMART, primarily as the company's executive representative.

3 As part of the UK Level 2 BIM standard, the government established a data exchange standard through its original data specification PAS 1192-2, subsequently superseded by BS EN ISO 19650. Within the PAS standard the requirement was to generate data in COBIE (Construction Operations Building Information Exchange) which is, in essence, a spreadsheet-based extraction of non-geometric data designed to expose certain characteristics of the underlying design. This is a complicated set of standards and interactions. A good place to start to understand them can be found at https://www.designingbuildings.co.uk/wiki/BIM_level_2 (accessed 12 June 2021).

4 This move can come none too soon, as construction is considered one of the least digitised (and productive) industries globally. See McKinsey Global Institute, 'Reinventing Construction: A Route to Higher Productivity' in *https://www.mckinsey.com/industries/capital-projects-and-infrastructure/our-insights/reinventing-construction-through-a-productivity-revolution*, ed. McKinsey & Company, McKinsey & Company, 2017.

5 https://www.buildingsmart.org/about/vision/ (accessed 11 June 2021).

6 Michael P. Gallaher, Alan C. O'Connor et al., 'Cost Analysis of Inadequate Interoperability in the U.S. Capital Facilities Industry', U.S. Department of Commerce Technology Administration, 2004.

7 Niraj Thurairajah and Dan Goucher, 'Advantages and Challenges of Using Bim: A Cost Consultant's Perspective', 49th Annual Associates Schools of Construction Conference, California Polytechnical State University, San Luis Obispo, California, 2013.

8 George Zarkadakis, '"Data Trusts" Could Be the Key to Better Ai' in *Harvard Business Review*, 2020, https://hbr.org/2020/11/data-trusts-could-be-the-key-to-better-ai (accessed 11 June 2021).

9 Kate Crawford, *Atlas of AI: Power, Politics, and the Planetary Costs of Artificial Intelligence*, Yale University Press, New Haven, CT, 2021, p 12.

10 'Veridical' meaning 'truthful, veracious, genuine', <https://www.merriam-webster.com/dictionary/veridical> (accessed 11 June 2021).

11 This research is described at length in Brian Christian, *The Alignment Problem: Machine Learning and Human Values*, W.W. Norton & Company, New York, 2020, pp 45 ff.

12 Timnit Gebru, Emily Bender, Angelina McMillan-Major and Margaret Mitchell, 'On the Dangers of Stochastic Parrots: Can Language Models Be Too Big?' in *FaccT '21*, Virtual, Canada, 2021.

13 Crawford, *op. cit.*, Chapter One 'Earth', pp 23 ff.

3.3

1 This robot was Doxel's first iteration for such a process. In subsequent version, the company developed a technology called VSLAM (vision-based simultaneous localisation and mapping) that is much less expensive and easier for construction managers to deploy. Email correspondence between the author and Kevin Ferguson of Doxel, 30 September 2021 and https://www.doxel.ai/post/360-degree-cameras-vslam (accessed 30 September 2021).

2 'BuildTech' is the term now generally accepted to refer to emergent digital technology in the built asset marketplace. See 'What does BuildTech mean?', <https://www.archdaily.com/924827/what-does-buildtech-mean (accessed 11 June 2021).

3 'AI Powered Project Controls', <https://www.doxel.ai/#press> (accessed 12 June 2021).

4 Royal Institute of British Architects, 'Standard Professional Services Contract 2020: Architectural Services', RIBA, London, 2020, p 41.

5 American Institute of Architects, 'B101-2017 Standard Form of Agreement between Owner and Architect', American Institute of Architects, Washington, DC, 2017, Sub-paragraph 3.6.2.1, p 9.

6 'Facebook's VC Backs new Doxel—AI and Computer Vision to Disrupt Construction Industry', *Architosh*, <https://architosh.com/2018/01/facebooks-vc-backs-new-doxel-ai-and-computer-vision-to-disrupt-construction-industry/> (accessed 16 September 2021).

7 See discussions in Chapter 2.4 about FRDM.org.

8 Niraj Thurairajah and Dan Goucher, 'Advantages and Challenges of Using BIM: A Cost Consultant's Perspective' in *49th Annual Associates Schools of Construction Conference*, California Polytechnical State University, San Luis Obispo, California, 2013.

9 While these conclusions are now being substantiated by firms outside the building industry like McKinsey, many of these concerns were defined by Roger Egan in Sir Roger Egan, 'Rethinking Construction: The Report of the Construction Task Force', 1998. In the US, statistics about conformance to budget and schedule range from 30% to 60% of projects failing to meet these goals.

10 Nicholas Negroponte, *The Architecture Machine*, MIT Press, Cambridge, MA, 1970.

11 'Foster + Partners and Boston Dynamics monitor construction with 'Spot' the robot dog', *Design Boom*, <https://www.designboom.com/architecture/foster-partners-boston-dynamics-construction-spot-robot-dog-11-11-2020/> (accessed 12 June 2021).

3.4

1 Deltek Clarity with Longitude, 'Deltek Clarity Architecture and Engineering Industry Study: Trends and Benchmarks in Emea and Apac' in *Annual Comprehensive Reports*, Deltek, 2021.

2 Architects' Council of Europe with Mirza & Nacey Research, 'The Architectural Profession in Europe 2020', 2021.

3 Construction Documents is typically 35% of the basic fee, and Construction Contract Administration another 20%. Some large portion of this effort is likely to be automated. The question whether that work is replaced with something of more value will be addressed in Chapter 3.5: Value Propositions and Business Models.

4 Daniel Susskind, *A World without Work: Technology, Automation and How We Should Respond*, Metropolitan Books/Henry Holt & Company, New York, 2020, pp 37 ff.

5 'The Architectural Profession in Europe 2020'.

6 According to the Architects' Council of Europe, 97% of firms in Europe have 10 or fewer staff.

7 See 'Construction jobs BOOM: Bricklayers and plasterers earn MORE than architects' at <https://www.express.co.uk/news/uk/930079/UK-jobs-construction-salary-bricklayers-electrician-plumbers-career-university> (accessed 12 June 2021).

8 See 'Architects who don't pay interns "shouldn't be given prestigious commissions" says designer who revealed Ishigami internships' at <https://www.dezeen.com/2019/03/25/architects-unpaid-internship-serpentine-pavilion/> (accessed 12 June 2021).

9 Peggy Deamer, *The Architect as Worker: Immaterial Labor, the Creative Class, and the Politics of Design*, Bloomsbury Academic, London and New York, 2015.

10 See '"I'm not a robot": Amazon workers condemn unsafe, grueling conditions at warehouse' at <https://www.theguardian.com/technology/2020/feb/05/amazon-workers-protest-unsafe-grueling-conditions-warehouse> (accessed 28 October 2021)

11 Timnit Gebru, Emily Bender, Angelina McMillan-Major and Margaret Mitchell, 'On the Dangers of Stochastic Parrots: Can Language Models Be Too Big?' in *FacT '21*, Virtual, Canada, 2021.

3.5

1 George Barnett Johnston, *Assembling the Architect: The History and Theory of Professional Practice*, Bloomsbury Visual Arts, London, 2020, p 117, quoting Frederick Squires and Rockwell Kent, *Architec-Tonics: The Tales of Tom Thumtack, Architect*, The William T. Comstock Company, New York, 1914.

2 Ibid., p 119.

3 An important distinction between, say, AIA and RIBA guidance on architectural fees stems from several lawsuits brought against the former by the US Department of Justice in the 1980s and 1990s, where standard fee schedules, still available from RIBA guidelines, were deemed to be anti-competitive. The AIA has therefore removed itself entirely from any discussions whatsoever of fees.

4 Nicolas G. Carr, 'It Doesn't Matter' in *Harvard Business Review*, 2003, <https://hbr.org/2003/05/it-doesnt-matter> (accessed 11 June 2021).

5 Many US architects report that, despite the slow recovery from the 2007–09 crisis, while fee volume has returned to pre-crisis levels (at least prior to Covid), fee contractions have yet to return from pre-crisis levels.

6 Ibid., p 117.

7 For a more detailed explanation of the course and its outputs, see Phil Bernstein, 'The Distractions of Disruptions: Technical Supply in an Era of Social Demand' in *Architectural Design (AD)*, 90, no. 02, 2020.

8 Lance Hosey, 'Going Beyond the Punchlist: Why Architects Should Embrace Post-Occupancy Evaluations', *Metropolis*, 2019, <https://www.metropolismag.com/architecture/architecture-post-occupancy-evaluations/> (accessed 15 June 2021).

9 Harvey M. Bernstein, 'Managing Uncertainty and Expectations in Building Design and Construction' in *McGraw Hill Smart Market Reports*, ed. Harvey M. Bernstein, McGraw Hill Construction Analytics, New York, 2014, p 12.

10 Ibid., p 29.

11 Hosey, *op cit*.

CONCLUSION

1 Arthur I. Miller, *The Artist in the Machine: The World of AI Powered Creativity*, MIT Press, Cambridge, MA, 2019, p 5.

2 Recently, a collective of UK architects has expressed strong misgivings about Autodesk's lagging development of the flagship BIM platform, Revit. See Daniel Davis, 'Architects Versus Autodesk' *Architect Magazine*, 27 August 2020.

3 BIM Industry Working Group, 'Bim Management for Value, Cost & Carbon Improvement: A Report for the Government Construction Client Group', UK Government Department of Business, Innovation and Skills, London March 2011.

4 Issues of forced labour and modern slavery were explored in a seminar taught at Yale in autumn 2020. See <https://www.architecture.yale.edu/courses/20242-fighting-slavery-in-the-building-supply-chain> (accessed 11 July 2021).

5 See Phillip G. Bernstein, 'A Way Forward? Integrated Project Delivery', *Harvard Design Magazine*, Spring 2010.

6 A typical example is the alleged uselessness of the architect's building information models for construction. Those data are created to fulfil the architect's requirement to define design intent, and lack the additional construction logic and detail that builders require to complete their work.

7 See Phillip G Bernstein. *Architecture Design Data: Practice Competency in the Era of Computation*, Birkhäuser, Basel, 2018.

8 Eyal Weizman, *Forensic Architecture: Violence at the Threshold of Detectability*, Zone Books; The MIT Press, Brooklyn, NY and Cambridge, MA, 2017, p 9.

9 This issue (and the example cited) is explored at length in Brian Christian, *The Alignment Problem: Machine Learning and Human Values*, 1st edn, W.W. Norton & Company, New York, 2020, Chapter 3., pp 82 ff.

10 Garrett Jacobs and Deanna Van Buren, 'Designing to Divest', *Architectural Record*, 5 October 2020, p 37.

INDEX

IMAGE CREDITS